Physical Education Self-Management for Healthy, Active Lifestyles

JEFF CARPENTER

Human Kinetics

Library of Congress Cataloging-in-Publication Data

Carpenter, Jeff.
  Physical education self-management for healthy, active lifestyles / Jeff Carpenter.
    p. cm.
  ISBN-13: 978-0-7360-6362-3 (soft cover)
  ISBN-10: 0-7360-6362-5 (soft cover)
  1. Physical education for children. I. Title.
  GV443.C376 2007
  372.86--dc22

                    2006022695

ISBN-10: 0-7360-6362-5
ISBN-13: 978-0-7360-6362-3

Copyright © 2007 by Jeff Carpenter

The Web addresses cited in this text were current as of December 2006, unless otherwise noted.

Acquisitions Editor: Scott Wikgren; **Developmental Editor:** Ragen E. Sanner; **Assistant Editors:** Carmel Sielicki, Bethany J. Bentley, and Anne C. Rumery; **Special Projects Editor:** Jeff King; **Copyeditor:** Annette Pierce; **Proofreader:** Julie Marx Goodreau; **Permission Manager:** Dalene Reeder; **Graphic Designer:** Fred Starbird; **Graphic Artist:** Dawn Sills; **Photo Manager:** Laura Fitch; **Cover Designer:** Keith Blomberg; **Photographer (cover):** Sarah Ritz; **Photographer (interior):** © Human Kinetics, except where otherwise noted; **Art Manager:** Kelly Hendren; **Illustrator:** Station diagrams and illustrations on "Motivators: What Motivates Me?"; "Influences: People Who Have Influenced My Life"; "Goal-Setting Practice Activity 2: Can I Achieve My Goals?"; "This Is Your Community"; and "Using My Resources" work sheets by Keri Evans; **Printer:** United Graphics

Printed in the United States of America   10 9 8 7 6 5 4 3 2 1

Human Kinetics
Web site: www.HumanKinetics.com

United States: Human Kinetics
P.O. Box 5076
Champaign, IL 61825-5076
800-747-4457
e-mail: humank@hkusa.com

Canada: Human Kinetics
475 Devonshire Road Unit 100
Windsor, ON N8Y 2L5
800-465-7301 (in Canada only)
e-mail: orders@hkcanada.com

Europe: Human Kinetics
107 Bradford Road
Stanningley
Leeds LS28 6AT, United Kingdom
+44 (0) 113 255 5665
e-mail: hk@hkeurope.com

Australia: Human Kinetics
57A Price Avenue
Lower Mitcham, South Australia 5062
08 8372 0999
e-mail: liaw@hkaustralia.com

New Zealand: Human Kinetics
Division of Sports Distributors NZ Ltd.
P.O. Box 300 226 Albany
North Shore City
Auckland
0064 9 448 1207
e-mail: info@humankinetics.co.nz

Physical Education Self-Management for Healthy, Active Lifestyles

To Nichole and all the other young children in hopes that they will gain the knowledge and skill to live healthy and active lifestyles, and to Jonathan for his patience and understanding in teaching me the true meaning of physical activity—to enjoy the simple act of participation.

Contents

Activity Finder

Activity name	Page number	Standards	Handouts available on CD-ROM
Chapter 2—Raising the Curtain on a Lifetime of Health and Fitness			
Motivation	17	PE 5 HE 1, 5	Motivators: What Motivates Me?
Reinforcement	20	PE 5 HE 1, 5	Reinforcers: Things That Help Accomplish a Goal
Influences on Healthy Behaviors	22	PE 5 HE 1, 2	Influences: People Who Have Influenced My Life
Positive Problem Solving	24	PE 5 HE 1, 5	Positive Problem Solving: Being Creative
Procrastination	27	PE 5 HE 5, 6	Procrastination: Time Provides Opportunities to Create Success
Goal Setting	30	PE 5 HE 6	• Goal-Setting Practice Activity 1: My Fitness Goal • Goal-Setting Practice Activity 2: Can I Achieve My Goals?
Community Resources	35	PE 5 HE 3	This Is Your Community
Chapter 3—Rehearsal for Lifelong Health and Physical Activity			
Basketball Skill Challenges and Motivators	39	PE 1, 2, 3 HE 4, 7	• Skill Challenge Checklists -Beginning level -Intermediate level -Advanced level • Station Motivator Cards
Soccer Skill Challenges and Motivators	50	PE 1, 2, 3 HE 4, 7	• Skill Challenge Checklists -Beginning level -Intermediate level -Advanced level • Station Motivator Cards

(continued)

(continued)

Preface

This book could be one of the most meaningful resources you will use in developing health and fitness programs to enhance the abilities of students in intermediate grades or middle students (students age 9 to 14) to assume control and responsibility for a healthy and active lifestyle. This book does not present specific skill-development or game activities. Rather, it provides a progression of activities that have proven successful in teaching students the skills and information they need to be able to set and manage their personal health and fitness goals.

Key principles noted in the Centers for Disease Control and Prevention's *Guidelines for School and Community Programs to Provide Lifelong Physical Activity Among Young People,* 1997, clearly state that physical education programs are most likely to meet current and future needs of young people if they include the following:

- Numerous physical activities that can be done throughout life, emphasize participation, and are enjoyable
- Opportunities to develop the necessary knowledge, motor and behavioral skills, attitudes, and confidence to adopt and maintain a healthy and active lifestyle
- A range of individual, dual, and team rhythmic activities appropriate for the age and developmental levels of the students taking part
- A coordinated effort between classroom-based health education, community-based programs and resources, and families.

To implement programs that meet national, state, and local outcomes, planners and teachers must recognize the roles that student motivation and positive attitudes play in student success. Teachers can encourage positive attitudes by providing students with programs that are enjoyable, meet their interests and needs, emphasize individual health benefits, and use active teaching and learning methods, which support positive student activity patterns.

Standards

Today, all high-quality educational programs are aligned with state and local standards, which are based on recognized national standards developed by the National Association for Sport and Physical Education. The following are the national standards adopted for physical education and health education. Although these national standards are, by design, written in general terms, they form the basis for more specific state, school district, building, and departmental standards, which in turn define the curriculum presented to students and corresponding assessments. Remember, standards are developed in a downward fashion—national to daily lesson—but are assessed upward: Each daily lesson must meet the various standards established at each ascending level.

NATIONAL STANDARDS FOR PHYSICAL EDUCATION

Standard 1

Demonstrates competency in motor skills and movement patterns needed to perform a variety of physical activities.

Standard 2

Demonstrates understanding of movement concepts, principles, strategies, and tactics as they apply to the learning and performance of physical activities.

Standard 3

Participates regularly in physical activity.

Standard 4

Achieves and maintains a health-enhancing level of physical fitness.

Standard 5

Exhibits responsible personal and social behavior that respects self and others in physical activity settings.

Standard 6

Values physical activity for health, enjoyment, challenge, self-expression, and/or social interaction.

Reprinted from *Moving Into the Future: National Standards for Physical Education,* 2nd Edition (2004) reprinted with permission from the National Association for Sport and Physical Education (NASPE), 1900 Association Drive, Reston, VA 20191, USA.

NATIONAL HEALTH EDUCATION STANDARDS

Standard 1

Students will comprehend concepts related to health promotion and disease prevention to enhance health.

Standard 2

Students will analyze the influence of family, peers, culture, media, technology, and other factors on health behaviors.

Standard 3

Students will demonstrate the ability to access valid information and products and services to enhance health.

Standard 4

Students will demonstrate the ability to use interpersonal communication skills to enhance health and avoid or reduce health risks.

Standard 5

Students will demonstrate the ability to use decision-making skills to enhance health.

Standard 6

Students will demonstrate the ability to use goal-setting skills to enhance health.

Standard 7

Students will demonstrate the ability to practice health-enhancing behaviors and avoid or reduce health risks.

Standard 8

Students will demonstrate the ability to advocate for personal, family, and community health.

Using This Book

This book focuses on intermediate grades and middle school programs, providing students age 9 to 14 with a scope of relevant activities. At the same time, it aims to expand an educator's understanding of how to define and measure success, improve student confidence, and increase student motivation and interest in physical activity. General program recommendations as well as the specific student-centered activities, work sheets, and assessments provided throughout this book challenge teachers to plan, personalize, and provide purposeful programs for all students.

The book is organized in six chapters that build on the concepts presented in the previous chapters.

Chapter 1 provides concepts and proven techniques to motivate students through self-management, goal setting, and self-assessment. Teaching students how to manage their environment, learn new skills, and provide rewards for themselves starts them down the path of developing a healthy lifestyle.

Chapter 2 provides student-centered activities that help students understand the issues and processes related to developing a healthy and active lifestyle: motivation, goal setting, and development of positive attitudes and personal confidence.

Chapter 3 continues the progression with skill development and practice activities that motivate and challenge students. The individual and group skill challenges provide students with the opportunity to move at their own rate by using a task-card system, allowing students to learn self-management techniques while increasing their physical abilities.

Chapter 4 focuses on problem solving and self-direction within the context of developing and maintaining a healthy and active lifestyle. The activities and resources presented provide each student with multiple opportunities to acquire new knowledge and learn new skills in addition to monitoring current and future activity and lifestyle patterns while planning for future activities.

Chapter 5 continues the progression toward self-management by focusing on clear guidelines and numerous challenging and enjoyable activities that will help students set personal goals. These activities consist of lessons and projects for both the entire class and for individuals.

Chapter 6 reviews previously presented information and skills that facilitate self-management and provides a step-by-step strategy for designing a personal health and fitness plan and for achieving the goals stated in the plan.

Most physical education programs effectively present health and fitness knowledge and develop physical skills. However, students often have trouble taking what they have learned and applying it outside the

PE class. This book fills that gap between school-directed programs and a lifetime of physical activity. As a professional educator, it should be your intent to motivate students to become healthy and active. To accomplish this, you must accept the fact that all students are individuals and, as such, assist them in developing knowledge and physical skills along with the ability to apply the skills of goal setting and self-management. This will increase their potential to develop and maintain a healthy and active lifestyle.

Final Thoughts for Success

When thinking about all the classes you've taken, which ones do you think helped you 5, 10, 15, or 20 years later? If you ask this question of teachers outside the field of health and fitness, they most likely will say it was math, English, technology, business, or science—not a physical education class. Many students believe their traditional physical education classes are a waste of time. However, at the same time, health and fitness professionals are pushing harder than ever to include more health-related physical activity and health-related knowledge in the daily lives of school-age children. To meet this challenge and provide meaningful experiences for all students, programs must include more than playing basketball or soccer.

Health experts believe that health and fitness education in school is necessary in order for students to understand the importance of frequent exercise and physical activity after graduation. This requires a new focus for your programs: to offer students more opportunities to develop a sound knowledge and skill base on which to build a lifetime of meaningful and enjoyable activity.

The goal of health and fitness eduation is to help students become more active and to see that physical activity can be fun as well as helpful in leading a healthy life now and in the future. Physical educators have a tremendous responsibility—facilitating the health of a future generation. Effective physical educators take this responsibility and meet its challenges each and every day.

Acknowledgments

In more than 35 years of professional experience I have had the opportunity to work with many people who have educated, influenced, and helped me learn and grow. At the top of the list is my son, Jonathan, who has shown me how to set lofty goals, overcome numerous barriers, and become a true champion. I am also grateful to Diane Tunnell, Jon Sunderland, Bud Turner, Kelly Rankin, and Bob Melson for advice and wise counsel over the years in helping to shape my philosophy and sense of professionalism. Finally, I am forever indebted to the thousands of students I have had the pleasure of working with; I believe I have learned more from them than they could ever have learned from me.

Setting the Stage for a Lifetime of Health and Fitness

© Image Source

© Photodisc

No matter who you are
or what you do, you have
the power to make
positive changes in your life.

ncluding physical activity in their daily lives can help adolescents
establish a healthy and active lifestyle now and in the future. However, many students are not physically active; do not have the tools to develop, implement, and monitor an active lifestyle; and have not developed a personal action plan for maintaining a healthy and active lifestyle. School-based physical education programs are essential for helping students acquire the knowledge and skills necessary for setting achievable goals, developing a personal action plan, and maintaining a healthy and active lifestyle.

Motivating for Success— Moving Toward Self-Management

Rather than teaching students ways to motivate and manage themselves, educators often use various methods to make students comply with their ideas. Generally, intermediate grades and middle school level students are maligned for their immaturity and impulsiveness and as a result are denied opportunities for self-management. Teaching students self-management skills and providing a curricular format in which they can practice these skills increase the students' internal motivation and encourage them to take responsibility for managing their lives.

National, state, and local standards set forth the goal of developing students who will actively participate in activities that teach them how to adopt and maintain a healthy and active lifestyle. If physical educators are to achieve this goal, they must set the stage by providing opportunities for goal setting and self-management. Although some students exhibit internal control and are self-motivated and self-managed, others do not have these skills. Some students need to begin the process with small goals and frequent rewards, while others who have a greater sense of internal control can make independent decisions. Rather than relying on chronological age to determine curriculum and programs, you can ask several questions about individual behavior and previous experience.

- Has the student demonstrated the ability to successfully participate in teacher-selected activities and progressions?
- Has the student made class decisions that are safe for himself and others?
- Has the student demonstrated the ability to learn from her mistakes?
- Has the student demonstrated the knowledge and skills necessary for making corrections that will lead to success?

When you have answered these questions for each student, you will have a sound basis on which to implement instructional methods and techniques that will encourage students to actively participate and fulfill their potential.

Learning to Set Goals

Self-management and self-motivation begin when a student learns to set goals. Because most students are accustomed to following and expected to follow the teacher's lead, their self-management skills are lacking. Although tricky, setting a goal is essential to successfully developing a personal health and fitness plan that will lead to an active and healthy lifestyle. Many students, and adults, quickly identify general end goals in a moment of optimism: "I'll run 5 miles (8 km) every day," or "I'll lose 20 pounds (9 kg) in two months." Teachers need to help students learn to set realistic goals by discussing specific expectations.

- Jamal has been inactive both in class and outside. He has decided to set a goal of running 5 miles (8 km) each day for the next three weeks to increase his aerobic fitness and receive extra credit for class. Is Jamal's goal realistic? (No)
- Rosa wants to lose 40 pounds (18 kg). She usually consumes 3,500 calories a day and gets little exercise. Her goal is to eat only one meal per day for the next six weeks and to run 1 mile (1.6 km) each day. Is Rosa's goal realistic? (No)
- Jon wants to improve his aerobic fitness level. He actively participates in class activities and rides his bike to school twice a week, which takes about 5 minutes each way. He wants to set a goal of continuing to be active in class, riding his bike to school three days per week, and walking two days. In addition, Jon will jog for 20 minutes three days per week. Is Jon's goal realistic? (Yes)

Teachers need to work with each student to set goals slightly beyond their current performance or achievement level. Goals should first span short periods of time, maybe only one or two class periods. Students also need to write their goals in measurable terms so that assessing progress is easy. If Alex is rarely active in class, his initial goal might be to actively participate in all activities for one week.

Once a goal is written, students need to record each day's progress: "How long did I jog today?" "What was my caloric intake?" Although most students accurately record data, teachers and family members initially may need to help in order to ensure accuracy. In addition, most students will need help in objectively observing their progress. Teachers should use various instructional tools, such as videotaping, peer observations, or simply recording check marks on an observation sheet, to help students in these self-observations.

Rewarding Your Accomplishments

After learning to set realistic goals and to monitor and assess their progress, students need to learn how to reward themselves for their accomplishments. Traditionally, the teacher, either through positive oral comments or grades, rewards students for progress. To help students manage their program, ask them which incentives will help them maintain their daily efforts. Remember, rewards can never be too frequent in the initial stages of a program. A common mistake is to set goals too high with rewards too small and too far between. To help your students, ask them to write down their daily rewards as they move toward their ultimate goal. For example, you might say to a student, "Good job today. What are you doing for yourself?" Ask students to write down their accomplishment, and reward and check their sheet daily, being sure to congratulate them.

Keep in mind that students may not achieve all their goals. Rather than penalizing themselves, students should learn that these situations are a part of the process. Short-term goals can be viewed as intermediate steps that need to be modified while keeping the ultimate goal in sight. For example, Sally has an ultimate goal of losing 15 pounds (6.75 kg) in six months. Her plan includes daily exercise through physical education classes supplemented by walking 30 minutes each day and eating a healthy diet. Her daily goal includes eating only three meals per day and one afternoon snack. On Tuesday she missed breakfast because she got up late. Rather than penalizing herself, Sally should look at the cause and determine what she can do in order to get up on time and eat breakfast.

She can also reward herself for doing her exercise and eating the other meals on schedule.

Essential Elements for Self-Management and Self-Motivation

If students are to become self-managed and self-motivated, they need to make sure they accomplish all essential elements of their plan. Ask each student to answer these questions. All answers should be yes. If a student answers no, discuss the reasons and help him or her modify the plan so that progress can continue.

- Did you allow enough time to accomplish your short-term goals?
- Did you have the knowledge and skill to accomplish your goals?
- Did you set up a progression of short-term goals?
- Did you set your short-term goals slightly beyond your current level?
- Did you set goals that are within your control and not dependent - on others?
- Did you write down your short-term and ultimate goals?
- Did you record your daily accomplishments?
- Did you reward yourself for your accomplishments?
- Did you increase your goals slowly after your success?
- Did you have someone to discuss your goals, activities, and rewards with?
- Did you try new skills for the first time with supportive people who could help you?
- Did you monitor and modify progress toward your daily and ultimate goals?
- Did you keep your ultimate goal in focus?

If students are to become self-managed and self-motivated, they need a supportive instructional environment that encourages individual tasks and goal setting within the context of high-quality physical education. Students continue to state that supportive teachers who provide direction are instrumental in helping them become independent learners and achievers.

Developing a Positive Attitude Toward Health and Activity

The educational reform movement has given new direction to physical education. There has been a surge of interest in developing innovative delivery systems and curricular programs that will motivate all students toward the development of a healthy and active lifestyle.

Perhaps the greatest change brought about by educational reform is its focus on intentional student outcomes. And the greatest changes attributed to this focus are the following:

- From a teacher-driven to student-driven program
- From learning that takes place only in class to learning that takes place throughout the school and community
- From a program accountable to itself to one that is accountable to students, parents, and the community
- From a program that is an end to itself to one that sets the stage for continued learning
- From a program that dictates the pace of learning to one that centers on the progress of the individual student
- From a "how to do it" curriculum that focuses on *what* to an inclusive curriculum that places equal emphasis on *what, why,* and *how.*
- From standards that are arbitrary to standards that focus on success by ensuring a positive and productive learning environment.

As school staff and their communities develop student-centered programs that take into account the changes just noted, they will develop and implement sufficiently challenging programs. These programs will address the areas of personal health-related fitness, movement competency, creativity in individual expression, and communication while promoting self-understanding, motivation, and confidence.

Developing Personal Confidence— Self-Fulfilling Prophecies

A self-fulfilling prophecy is a preconceived expectation that affects the way people achieve success. Because your expectation affects the way you behave toward students, it can cause your initial prophecy to come true. Teachers are often unaware of their initial expectations and how preconceptions alter their conduct.

Examples of self-fulfilling prophecies are evident in most schools. Based on conversations with others or preconceived ideas regarding certain groups, a teacher may have low expectations for certain students. In turn, these low expectations are reflected in lesson planning and presentation methods. In some cases, they can result in lower achievement for a student and, ultimately, a lack of confidence in his or her ability to succeed.

Although research and best practices demonstrate the need to modify instruction and allow students to set achievable goals based on individual abilities, teachers must nevertheless realize that their preconceptions about a student inevitably alter their behavior. Rather than hamper a student's progress toward developing personal confidence and his or her ability to develop a healthy and active lifestyle, teachers must monitor their attitudes and conduct in an effort to create a consistently positive prophecy for all students.

Success Through Motivation

Not every student is attracted to the same activity or type of reward. Some students enjoy an activity because participation brings them pleasure or satisfaction. They are intrinsically motivated. However, every student will not be intrinsically motivated by every activity. When an activity is not intrinsically motivating, students rely on external, or extrinsic, rewards. These extrinsic rewards often provide the motivation to work at a task that they do not perceive as necessary or rewarding.

The goal of a comprehensive health and fitness program is to develop the students' desire to participate in activities in order to live a healthy, enjoyable, and productive life. Teachers do this by presenting the appropriate and necessary knowledge and skills to all students. Although teachers cannot intrinsically motivate students to use the information and skills, they can create an environment in which students are free to set personal goals, are given the freedom to choose from a variety of activities, and are able to develop the ability to monitor their own progress.

Programs that foster a student's desire to participate in physical activities are built around instructional activities that provide numerous opportunities for success. They also include intentional-learning experiences that ensure the attainment of individual outcomes. Remember, students need to work at their own level, achieve success, and avoid extended periods of frustration. Students who are successful will progress and gain satisfaction from their experiences.

Power of Praise

The simple act of praising desirable behaviors and individual achievement motivates most students. Individual and specific praise is probably the most powerful, yet most ignored, motivator teachers can provide students. Both underachievers and the talented are responsive and sensitive to praise.

Praise must be genuine, individual, specific, and nonevaluative. At times, compliments that are general and sound like an evaluation or those that pressure students to repeat superior performances may create a fear of failure. Comments such as "You did a great job today in aerobics. Do you feel closer to accomplishing your aerobic fitness goal?" are much better received than "You did a great job today. Let's see you do it again tomorrow."

Remember, be genuine, individual, specific, and nonevaluative. This is not only motivational but also helps the student gain confidence in his or her ability to create a healthy lifestyle.

Instructional Success

The major difference between today's health and fitness programs and those of 10 years ago lies in the focus on the individual student and the emphasis on self-direction. A successful program guarantees each student maximal involvement in relevant activities and learning experiences.

Instructors must use different teaching styles that include teacher-led, student-directed, and individualized activities. The problem-solving method also becomes an important instructional approach when students develop their personal health and fitness plans.

Class Organization and Management

Research and best practices clearly indicate that teachers who organize and manage their classes through activity not only manage instructional time and student behavior more easily but also facilitate higher levels of student learning. Teachers must not only plan the activities but also must teach students routines and how to take responsibility for participating in instruction and practice. When students take this responsibility, they also develop self-motivation and self-direction.

In presenting class lessons in an efficient manner, teachers set the stage for what they want students to be able to do outside of class. Therefore, the tone of the lesson must be established as soon as the students enter the facility. The amount of time typically spent at the beginning of a class for administrative or managerial tasks often slows or even stops the lesson. However, when students participate in activities outside of the class, they either have already planned them or are informed of the activity and they simply begin.

One way to get things moving and to reduce the time spent on administrative tasks is to post information about the activities that students are expected to do when they enter the class. Post the information in a place that students will see when they enter the facility. If the students need to change clothes, a spot in the locker room near the exit door works well. If the students come straight to the gym without changing, place the information on a bulletin board near the entrance. The information should include what students should do when they enter the gym and what activity will be presented.

Letting students know what is expected gives them the opportunity to prepare and think about what they must do. They take responsibility for management and being prepared. This procedure frees teachers from using instructional time to give simple directions.

Instructional Objective

An objective describes a proposed change in a student. It states what the student will know and be able to do after he or she has successfully completed the instructional process.

Teachers preparing instructional objectives is similar to students setting realistic goals for accomplishing a stated outcome. The first step in the process is to decide on the goals that students should achieve at the end of the program. Today, these "exit" outcomes most likely have been set by the state or district (e.g., students will develop, implement, and monitor a personal health and fitness plan). After the exit outcome is determined, the teacher must select procedures, content, and methods that are relevant to the objective and help students measure their progress toward meeting the objective.

Programs that provide students with the opportunity to be self-managed and self-motivated state specific learner objectives in terms different than those in traditional objective statements. Traditionally, objectives state the activities that students will perform to meet a program goal. In a self-managed program, teachers state the exit outcome of the program and provide numerous activities and pathways to achieve the outcome.

Stating the Standard

In addition to stating which goals and objectives your students must meet, you must describe how well you want the task performed. You must describe the criterion of acceptable performance.

If you specify the minimum acceptable performance for each objective, you will have a performance standard against which to assess performance. In addition to measuring the accomplishments of your students, stating the specific minimum criterion allows you to assess your instructional program and whether you have achieved the program goals.

For example, if one of your program goals is for students to be able to run one-half mile (800 m), and you do not intend to assess the student on the basis of time, you can state the objective as written. However, if you will not consider the objective accomplished unless students can run the distance in less than 3 minutes, it is only fair to let them know your intent: To be able to run one-half mile (800 m) in 3 minutes. The criterion is often stated informally when you tell students how much time is allowed.

In a self-managed program, students must know the specific criterion against which they will be measured. The best method for communicating this is to write the exit outcome and list the specific standard used to measure accomplishment. This allows the student to take this information and build a personal program designed to accomplish the stated objective.

Home and Community Partnerships

Throughout the years, educators have looked to their communities for support. To gain this support they have used student demonstrations, parent newsletters, and the print media to highlight instructional programs. Although communication is the cornerstone of community involvement, teachers need to take the next step in using the numerous resources within their community.

Enhancing Home Involvement

The implementation of quality programs requires a cooperative effort between educators and parents. Although parents may, at times, seem distant or negative, each has a desire to help his or her child develop a healthy lifestyle.

In recent years, physical educators have done this by addressing the specific needs of individual students, involving parents and family members in supporting the child's efforts to develop a healthy and active lifestyle, enhancing the home–school communication network related to health and fitness, and eliciting assistance from families to help meet the needs of the program.

To provide opportunities for parental and family involvement, teachers must take a proactive first step and remember that no matter which activity parents and family members participate in, it is important to maintain a positive attitude and be flexible. When moving beyond the traditional roles for parent and family involvement—assisting in classes, fitness testing, field days, and student programs—toward the role of supporting an individual student's self-management, teachers must look to additional avenues of involvement. These roles include the following:

- Assisting with health and fitness homework (e.g., monitoring activity journals, working with students on nutrition programs, and participating in family activity programs)
- Providing access to community resources
- Participating in ongoing communication with school staff
- Providing a supportive environment for student development of a healthy and active lifestyle

There are many ways to enhance home involvement in a student's physical education. Regardless of the way a family chooses, parents, families, and students will respond in a positive manner when presented with ongoing, student-centered information and positive/directed roles.

Reaching Out to the Community: Building Connections and Collaboration

The aim of outreach to the community is to develop greater involvement in the educational process and enhance support for students. Outreach may take two forms: first to bring the community into the schools and second to provide students access to community resources. Traditionally, schools have used a variety of community resources to provide specific information, for example, medical professionals speaking about disease prevention and police officers presenting information on personal safety. In programs designed to enhance self-management and the development of active and healthy lifestyles, teachers bring community members to schools to present their expertise in a specific activity and provide students information on how to use specific resources after school hours. An example of this form of involvement and collaboration is illustrated in the following unit example.

ACTIVE RECREATIONAL ACTIVITIES UNIT

This unit provides both classroom-based and community-based activities. Community resource personnel work in direct coordination with school staff to provide direct instruction during regularly scheduled class times. At the conclusion of school-based instruction, students take a series of field trips to participate in the community; in some cases these trips take place over a weekend.

(continued)

Active Recreational Activities Unit   *(continued)*

- Hiking and climbing: Contact a local climbing club to assist in instruction. On-site instruction includes safety, equipment, and technique. (Your school doesn't need a climbing wall. Many climbing clubs bring equipment that allows students to climb surfaces commonly found in most gymnasiums.) Practice hikes are taken around the school grounds and neighborhood during class times. Orienteering can also be a part of this component.
- Daylong field trips could include hikes at local parks or on hiking trails. Weekend trips could incorporate basic climbs and hikes and include camping.
- Boating and boating safety: Contact a local boating safety educational organization, such as Power Squadron, or the local rowing club, yacht club, or parks and recreation department to assist with instruction. On-site instruction includes boating and water safety, boating basics, and different forms of boating (rowing, sailing, kayaking, and canoeing). Off-site experiences include participation in various boating activities on local waters.
- Fitness resources: Contact local health clubs for help with instruction. Although many schools have specific fitness areas equipped with free weights, resistance machines, and aerobic equipment, the involvement of local clubs establishes a direct link between students and community resources. Health club professionals can provide students support and a different perspective. In addition, many clubs provide special discounts to students.
- Golf and tennis: Contact local Professional Golfers' Association of America (PGA) and United States Tennis Association (USTA) professionals to assist with instruction. Both organizations provide professional instruction and equipment to schools. These instructional field trips to golf courses and driving ranges and local tennis facilities provide not only exposure to the sports and basic instruction; they also provide a direct link to community resources.

Forming a professional collaborative relationship with community members provides positive support for your programs. And exposure to these facilities and resources also opens up a variety of activities to students that can help them develop their self-management and activity patterns.

Independent Studies

Although students should complete basic instruction during school hours, to fulfill the goal of self-management, you should also make available opportunities for independent study. At the elementary-school level these activities might be used for extra credit. At the secondary-school level, actual credit may be offered. To maintain the integrity of school programs, you must develop specific criteria for granting credit. The following procedure has proven effective and beneficial to students in their quest to demonstrate self-management and the independent use of the skills learned during their school-based health and fitness programs.

Students may request credit after completing basic instruction in health and fitness. Requests must include the following:

- Name of the program or learning experience they will participate in
- Length of time for the program
- Measurable objectives of the program, including specific goals and monitoring processes, a complete outline of activities they will participate in, direct relationship to the school-based health and fitness program, a complete description of how performance will be assessed (including periodic check-ins with school staff), and a signed agreement with a qualified community resource staff member to monitor the program or provide instruction. See the following example of a student request.

EXAMPLE OF A SPECIFIC STUDENT REQUEST

By completing individual or independent studies, students can demonstrate their ability to develop and manage personal health and fitness programs, thereby meeting one of the program's exit outcomes: to design and implement a personal health and fitness plan.
Independent study plan for _____

- **Goal**—To obtain one semester (.5 credit) of junior high school credit. I plan to spend 75 hours during the semester engaged in a directed activity.
- **Activity**—Lifetime activity through a jujutsu class offered at the South Area YMCA
- **Dates**—January 3 through May 29

(continued)

Example of a Specific Student Request   *(continued)*

- **Outline**—Jujutsu is a Japanese martial art. I will learn the various moves of jujutsu, including escapes and holds, throwing techniques, rolling and falling, striking, blocking, and grappling.
- **Objectives**—Learn the basic moves of jujutsu, demonstrate an understanding of the basics of jujutsu, and obtain feedback on progress from instructors.
- **Student learning objectives covered**—South District learning objectives 1.1, 3.1.2, 3.1.3, and 4.2
- **Assessment plan**—Direct oral and written feedback from YMCA instructor (Mr. Jon Anderson) and monthly meetings with Ms. Gimenez (MJH health and fitness department chair)

Approved by: _____ Date: _____

Teacher comments: _____

_____

_____

Teaching students self-management skills through a variety of program formats enhances the likelihood that they will pursue a healthy and active lifestyle in the future.

. . . .

Raising the Curtain on a Lifetime of Health and Fitness

Take charge of your health,
stick your neck out,
and learn something new.

Setting goals and ultimately achieving them gives students a sense of direction and control, which can lead to increased self-esteem and motivation and the continued pursuit of new goals. Although many teachers believe that students have mastered the goal-setting process and are motivated by teacher, school, or group goals, the fact remains that students need specific knowledge and skills before they can set personal goals, monitor their progress, and be motivated by internal factors. The following activities, along with corresponding class discussions, help students gain a better understanding of the issues and processes involved with motivation, goal setting, and the development of a positive attitude and personal confidence.

MOTIVATION

When students know what their motivators are and can express them, their performance and personal satisfaction increases.

STANDARDS

▶ Physical Education Standard 5: Exhibits responsible personal and social behavior that respects self and others in physical activity settings.

▶ Health Education Standard 1: Students will comprehend concepts related to health promotion and disease prevention to enhance health.

▶ Health Education Standard 5: Students will demonstrate the ability to use decision-making skills to enhance health.

GET READY

▶ Ask students what motivates them to participate in physical activities— why do they participate? Write down the general answers and be prepared to use them to begin class discussions.

▶ Duplicate the Motivators: What Motivates Me work sheet for students.

GET SET

On the board or a large sheet of paper, list the motivators students have shared with you. Before beginning discussions, ask the students to list their personal motivators on a sheet of paper, fold it, and place it in their pocket.

GO!

Begin a class discussion by talking to students about motivation and how different things motivate each of us to be active and to succeed in achieving a goal, some intrinsic and some extrinsic. Facilitate a class discussion related to personal motivators. As students begin to share, check off common motivators on your list. At the conclusion of the discussion, pass out the motivator work sheet and have students complete it. After about 10 minutes, have them compare their first list (in their pocket) with their work sheet and discuss the differences and why their thoughts may have changed.

◄ TEACHER HINT

This is a great activity for getting students to think about goals and motivation. Extensions to the activity include the following:

▶ Have students in groups of two or three create a collage with magazine pictures or symbols representing high and low motivators.

▶ Facilitate a discussion on what the pictures represent and why they were designated as high or low motivators.

▶ Ask the students which important people in their lives know what their high and low motivators are.

Name: _____ Date: _____

Motivators: What Motivates Me?

Rank each of the following from 1 to 10: 1 is the most motivating factor; 10 is the least motivating.

_____ Having fun   _____ Personal success

_____ Family or friends   _____ Being healthy and fit

_____ Controlling what I do   _____ Getting a reward

_____ Being popular   _____ Getting a high grade

_____ Being able to play sports   _____ Getting along with others

Why did you rank number 1 as high? _____

_____

Who can you tell that your number 1 is a high-ranking motivator? _____

What benefit would you get from telling someone about your high motivator?

_____

_____

_____

_____

_____

Why did you rank your number 10 as low?

_____

Who can you tell that your number 10 is a low-ranking motivator? _____

What benefit would you get from telling someone about your low motivator?

_____

_____

_____

_____

_____

REINFORCEMENT

It is important to recognize both external and internal motivators that students can use to help them achieve a task or goal. Combining the knowledge of what motivates students with an understanding of reinforcement will enhance their success and self-direction.

STANDARDS

▶ Physical Education Standard 5: Exhibits responsible personal and social behavior that respects self and others in physical activity settings.

▶ Health Education Standard 1: Students will comprehend concepts related to health promotion and disease prevention to enhance health.

▶ Health Education Standard 5: Students will demonstrate the ability to use decision-making skills to enhance health.

GET READY

Prepare a Reinforcers: Things That Help Accomplish a Goal work sheet for each student. Review the tasks listed on the work sheet and make a sample sheet, maybe using a personal goal or a task you want to accomplish.

GET SET

▶ Duplicate copies of your sample work sheet and be prepared to discuss the examples with the class.

▶ Review various forms of both internal motivation (self-motivation) and external motivation and how each is used to reinforce progress and achievement.

GO!

Begin the class discussion by giving examples of various reinforcements that traditionally motivate students. Ask which ones are internal and which are external. Can students give other examples of internal reinforcers? Give students a work sheet, ask them to complete the tasks, and discuss the results.

TEACHER HINT

An excellent way to begin the discussion of student work sheets is to read one anonymous example from various work sheets.

Name: _____ Date: _____

Reinforcers:
Things That Help Accomplish a Goal

List five tasks or goals you would like to accomplish. List the external and internal reinforcers that will help you accomplish the task or goal.

Task or goal	External reinforcer	Internal reinforcer
Example: I will exercise four days per week.	I will buy myself a treat after two days. I will go to a movie after the first week.	I will feel healthier. I will feel proud after accomplishing my goal.
1.		
2.		
3.		
4.		
5.		

From Jeff Carpenter, 2007, *Physical Education Self-Management for Healthy, Active Lifestyles* (Champaign, IL: Human Kinetics).

INFLUENCES ON HEALTHY BEHAVIORS

Many people influence the lives of students. These influences can be either positive or negative. This activity encourages students to take a look at the positive and negative influences people have had on their lives.

STANDARDS

▶ Physical Education Standard 5: Exhibits responsible personal and social behavior that respects self and others in physical activity settings.

▶ Health Education Standard 1: Students will comprehend concepts related to health promotion and disease prevention to enhance health.

▶ Health Education Standard 2: Students will analyze the influence of family, peers, culture, media, technology, and other factors on health behaviors.

GET READY

Review the student work sheet and add categories, if necessary. Duplicate enough copies for each student.

GET SET

Make a list of people who have influenced your life—what was it about them and how did they influence you—to use as an example during class discussion. Write the list on the board or a large sheet of paper.

GO!

1. See if students are influenced by individuals who display similar or different personal characteristics, roles, or professions. Discuss reasons for the similarities and differences.

2. Give students a work sheet to complete. After students complete the work sheet, see if there are consistencies among the lists. Discuss what makes these people influential.

Name: _____ Date: _____

Influences:
People Who Have Influenced My Life

Throughout your life, many people influence the decisions you make, activities you participate in, and goals you set. They may be members of your family, classmates, friends, or someone you have read or heard about.

Using this work sheet, list at least one person in each category, what about them influenced you, and how their influence has affected you. Take enough time to think about these influences carefully.

	Who are the people in my life?	What about them influenced me?	How did that influence me?
Family			
Friends			
Teachers			
Public figures			
Celebrities			
People in history			
Fictional characters			

From Jeff Carpenter, 2007, *Physical Education Self-Management for Healthy, Active Lifestyles* (Champaign, IL: Human Kinetics).

23

POSITIVE PROBLEM SOLVING

Often when confronted with a problem, it is difficult to see alternative solutions, options, and possibilities. This activity provides students with the opportunity to think creatively, recognize their choices, and improve their ability to solve problems.

STANDARDS

▶ Physical Education Standard 5: Exhibits responsible personal and social behavior that respects self and others in physical activity settings.

▶ Health Education Standard 1: Students will comprehend concepts related to health promotion and disease prevention to enhance health.

▶ Health Education Standard 5: Students will demonstrate the ability to use decision-making skills to enhance health

GET READY

▶ Prepare for a class discussion on problem solving by developing a list of age-appropriate, health-related issues facing students. One way to develop this list is to ask students what, if anything, concerns them about their health or fitness level.

▶ Prepare copies of the Positive Problem Solving: Being Creative work sheet for students.

GET SET

Arrange the class in groups of three or four and present each group with a specific problem to solve. Instruct them to cooperate and work together to come up with ways to solve the group's problem. Students must identify the problem, whether it can be solved, whether there are different ways to solve it, the best way to solve it, and how to begin taking action. Although this is done as a group activity, the process and creativity will carry over to individual problem solving.

GO!

Begin a class discussion by identifying a specific problem (e.g., I need more time to meet my aerobic exercise goal). Have each group discuss the issue and determine a way to achieve the goal of meeting an aerobic exercise goal. Give each student a work sheet to complete. After students complete the work sheet, facilitate a follow-up discussion.

◀ TEACHER HINT

After the class discussion and when the students have completed the work sheet, present a class activity in which students must solve a problem in order to succeed (e.g., mastering an obstacle course containing several challenges that require individual and group problem solving).

Name: _____ Date: _____

Positive Problem Solving: Being Creative

Identify a specific problem that you have encountered while trying to accomplish your health and fitness goals.

_____

_____

_____

_____

_____

_____

_____

_____

Be creative and list options and possible solutions.

_____ _____

_____ _____

_____ _____

_____ _____

_____ _____

_____ _____

Put an X by the solutions or options that seem reasonable.

Choose the three best options or solutions and state why you chose them.

1. _____

_____

2. _____

_____

3. _____

_____

PROCRASTINATION

Procrastination is an ineffective way to manage time, yet, at one time or another, everyone does it. Teaching students how to assess a task's relative priority and how to develop a personal action plan helps them deal with the tendency to delay action. This activity gives students the knowledge and skills necessary to analyze and set priorities and improves their time management skills.

STANDARDS

▶ Physical Education Standard 5: Exhibits responsible personal and social behavior that respects self and others in physical activity settings.

▶ Health Education Standard 5: Students will demonstrate the ability to use decision-making skills to enhance health.

▶ Health Education Standard 6: Students will demonstrate the ability to use goal-setting skills to enhance health.

GET READY

▶ One or two weeks before this lesson, watch students and staff to find examples of how people put things off until the last minute and how that affects their time management and ability to successfully accomplish a task. Make a list of these examples to share with the class.

▶ Make copies of the Procrastination: Time Provides Opportunities to Create Success work sheet for each student.

Teacher Note

When you make the list discussed in Get Ready, record behaviors only, not the names of the people who demonstrate the behaviors. After sharing your list, ask students if they have seen people exhibiting these or similar behaviors—remember, behaviors only. Add these behaviors to your list.

GET SET

Arrange the class in groups of three or four and ask them to think about what procrastination is and how it might affect their ability to complete a task. Students might answer that procrastination is waiting until the last minute to do an assignment or study for a test, and it keeps them from having enough time to do their best.

GO!

Discuss the concepts of setting priorities, time management, and procrastination. Have students give examples of how procrastination can prevent

27

them from achieving a specific task or a goal. Have students complete the procrastination work sheet.

◖ TEACHER HINT

1. After students have completed their work sheets, ask them to give examples of the tasks they find are most often affected by procrastination. Write these tasks on the board.

2. Divide students into small groups and ask them to use their problem-solving skills to develop a reasonable action plan for accomplishing the tasks listed. Review the positive benefits of productive time management.

Name: _____ Date: _____

Procrastination:
Time Provides Opportunities
to Create Success

List tasks or activities that you tend to put off and how you feel when you keep putting a task off. Determine if the task or activity is a priority; if it is, develop an action plan for accomplishing it.

Things I put off	How I feel	Is it a priority?	My action plan
		___ Yes ___ No	
		___ Yes ___ No	
		___ Yes ___ No	
		___ Yes ___ No	
		___ Yes ___ No	

From Jeff Carpenter, 2007, *Physical Education Self-Management for Healthy, Active Lifestyles* (Champaign, IL: Human Kinetics).

GOAL SETTING

It takes practice to write realistic and measurable goals. Students need reminders that goals are simply targets that can be modified based on a person's progress. This activity provides students with direct practice in setting goals by teaching them how to use three criteria: identify the task (what do I want to do?), identify the standard (how much or how well will I do it?), and identify the time frame (when do I want to accomplish this goal?).

STANDARDS

▶ Physical Education Standard 5: Exhibits responsible personal and social behavior that respects self and others in physical activity settings.

▶ Health Education Standard 6: Students will demonstrate the ability to use goal-setting skills to enhance health.

GET READY

▶ Before practicing goal setting by learning to use the three criteria listed—task, standard, and time frame—students need to understand what these criteria are and how they affect the intended outcomes.

▶ Duplicate the two goal-setting practice work sheets for each student.

GET SET

Discuss the need for setting realistic and measurable goals, writing them down, and reviewing them regularly. Follow that discussion with a review of the three criteria for writing goals—identifying a specific task, realistic and measurable standards, and a realistic time frame for accomplishment.

GO!

Ask each student to complete the first goal-setting practice work sheet, My Fitness Goal. Ask students to complete the work sheet in pencil to reinforce the concept that if a goal is not realistic, they can erase it and revise it. After completing the first work sheet, have the students list two additional goals they would like to achieve. When their list is complete, have them do the second work sheet, Can I Achieve My Goals?

TEACHER HINT

Ask students to read one or two of their goals. Write these goals on the board, seeing if more than one student has the same goal. Give examples of how people who share a goal can often work together to give each other support and encouragement.

Name: _____ Date: _____

I will reach my goal by: _____

Goal-Setting Practice Activity 1:
My Fitness Goal

Answer the following questions about your fitness goal. Remember, a goal must be specific, realistic, and measurable.

What is your fitness goal?

_____

_____

_____

_____

_____

_____

_____

How will you benefit from achieving your goal?

_____

_____

_____

_____

_____

_____

_____

How will you achieve your goal?

_____

_____

_____

_____

(continued)

From Jeff Carpenter, 2007, *Physical Education Self-Management for Healthy, Active Lifestyles* (Champaign, IL: Human Kinetics).

My Fitness Goal *(continued)*

_____

_____

_____

What might get in your way?

_____

_____

_____

_____

_____

_____

How can you overcome some of the things that are in your way?

_____

_____

_____

_____

_____

_____

Who can help you?

_____

_____

_____

_____

_____

_____

I will do my best to accomplish my goal. If I need help, I'll ask for it and keep working.

Student signature: _____

From Jeff Carpenter, 2007, *Physical Education Self-Management for Healthy, Active Lifestyles* (Champaign, IL: Human Kinetics).

Name: _____ Date: _____

Goal-Setting Practice Activity 2:
Can I Achieve My Goals?

Remember, a goal includes a task or activity you want to accomplish. You will need to know how to measure your progress and identify a specific amount of time for accomplishing your goal. When filling out the practice work sheet, include all three criteria.

Example: I will (task) do 20 minutes of aerobic activity (standard) three times per week for the (time frame) next two months.

It's Up to You

Goal 1

_____
_____
_____
_____
_____

Can you really achieve this goal? ____Yes ____No

How will you know when you've reached your goal?

_____
_____

(continued)

From Jeff Carpenter, 2007, *Physical Education Self-Management for Healthy, Active Lifestyles* (Champaign, IL: Human Kinetics).

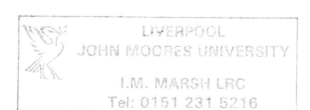
33

CD-ROM

Can I Achieve My Goals? *(continued)*

_____

_____

_____

Goal 2

_____

_____

_____

_____

_____

Can you really achieve this goal? ____Yes ____No

How will you know when you've reached your goal?

_____

_____

_____

_____

_____

Goal 3

_____

_____

_____

_____

Can you really achieve this goal? ____Yes ____No

How will you know when you've reached your goal?

_____

_____

_____

_____

From Jeff Carpenter, 2007, *Physical Education Self-Management for Healthy, Active Lifestyles* (Champaign, IL: Human Kinetics).

COMMUNITY RESOURCES

Health and fitness resources are available in all communities. Unfortunately, schools and students are often unaware of how to make use of them. Teaching students about these resources and how to use them can help them achieve their goals. The following activity increases your students' awareness of community resources that they may use to accomplish their individual goals.

STANDARDS

▶ Physical Education Standard 5: Exhibits responsible personal and social behavior that respects self and others in physical activity settings.

▶ Health Education Standard 3: Students will demonstrate the ability to access valid information and products and services to enhance health.

GET READY

▶ Research your community to find appropriate resources that provide on-site services and support or that students can have access to. Make a list of these resources to discuss with students.

▶ Duplicate the work sheet This Is Your Community for students.

GET SET

Present and discuss the community resource list. After this introductory class discussion, have students get into small groups. Ask each group to discuss these resources and place them in categories such as fitness centers, recreational activities, health services, and personal support. Have each group tell what category they placed each resource in.

GO!

Have students complete the work sheet. Make phone books and other community resource lists available or have students complete the work sheet as a homework assignment. After students have completed the work sheet, ask them to share the resources they have listed. Compare student lists.

TEACHER HINT

Review the importance of reinforcement and having family or friends to work with. After sharing individual resource lists, have students with similar goals work together to use the resources. Invite staff from various community resources to your class to talk about how students can use these resources.

Name: _____ Date: _____

This Is Your Community

Make a list of all community resources that are available for you to use when working on your health and fitness goals (e.g., fitness clubs, YMCA, golf courses, bowling centers, city parks, and recreation departments). If there are barriers to using these resources, list them and determine how to overcome the barriers.

Name of resource	Type of service	Address	Phone number
Example: Shape Up Fitness Center	Weight equipment and various group fitness classes	2273 Black Lake Road	555-1234

On a separate sheet of paper make a note of how you can use each of these resources to help you reach a personal health and fitness goal.

Rehearsal for Lifelong Health and Physical Activity

For true success in building
a healthy lifestyle
ask yourself three questions:
why? why not? why not now?

Students at all grade levels are motivated by a challenge; however, it is particularly important to provide individual challenges at the intermediate grades and middle school level. It is at this level of schooling that the basics of a self-management system are introduced. The activities in this chapter present self-management skills through individual challenges printed on station task cards. This method allows students to direct their own learning.

Skill Challenges and Motivators

In the following activities, students participate in a series of skill-based challenges, starting at a beginning level and progressing through a sequence of skills of increasing difficulty. All students start at the beginning level and proceed through the progression at their own pace. After completing the series, students will have refined their basic skills, learned new skills, and enhanced their eye–hand coordination, balance, and movement patterns.

This individually paced skill-development progression allows students to successfully move into the lead-up games and more formal activities that will use the specific skills acquired during the skill challenges.

BASKETBALL SKILL CHALLENGES AND MOTIVATORS

Basketball is an activity that can provide immediate rewards for individuals and teams. To build on a success-oriented format, selected activities should be fun and challenging: for example, "How many can you or your team do?" or by giving rewards for effort rather than scoring points.

STANDARDS

▶ Physical Education Standard 1: Demonstrates competency in motor skills and movement patterns needed to perform a variety of physical activities.

▶ Physical Education Standard 2: Demonstrates understanding of movement concepts, principles, strategies, and tactics as they apply to the learning and performance of physical activities.

▶ Physical Education Standard 3: Participates regularly in physical activity.

▶ Health Education Standard 4: Students will demonstrate the ability to use interpersonal communication skills to enhance health and avoid or reduce health risks.

▶ Health Education Standard 7: Students will demonstrate the ability to practice health-enhancing behaviors and avoid or reduce health risks.

GET READY

▶ Set up one station for each skill challenge. Make sure there is enough room at the Spot Shot station so that students rebounding the ball don't interfere with other stations. On the first day of the challenge, set up stations only for the beginning level. As students begin to progress, provide stations for all levels.

▶ If there aren't enough basketballs for all stations, use playground balls or volleyballs at the passing stations.

▶ Duplicate a skill challenge checklist for each student.

GET SET

▶ Demonstrate each of the challenge skills at the beginning level.

▶ Arrange students in pairs and distribute the equipment for each task. If you have an odd number of students, use groups of three with students rotating practice times.

GO!

1. Ask all groups to begin practicing the skill for the beginning level of the first challenge. Not all students will successfully complete the challenges at the same time or at the same level.

2. Students work at each station for 2 minutes. As groups accomplish a challenge, they should check it off their skill challenge sheet. Before rotating to the next station, students do 15 to 20 seconds of push-ups or curl-ups and then jog one lap around the area and stop at the station to the right of the one they just completed. Spot check the sheets and give students appropriate feedback to keep them on track.

3. If students have difficulty accomplishing a task, have them demonstrate a lower-level skill, then break the new skill into small components, giving them time to practice each. If, after practicing for a while, a student cannot meet the established goal but can meet part of it, note the accomplishment on the challenge sheet and let the student move on.

4. To increase motivation and add practice stations, place alternative challenge stations in the rotation. These stations can include juggling, jump rope tricks, and various fitness challenges.

STATIONS

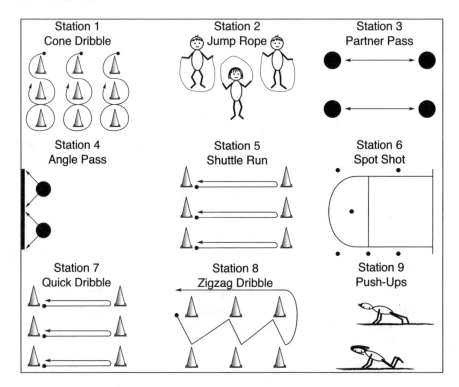

▶ Station 1, Cone Dribble—Set three cones approximately 4 feet (1.2 m) apart. On the go signal, begin dribbling around the cones—passing the first cone on the right, the second on the left, and so on.

▶ Station 2, Jump Rope—Students jump rope using any step or technique they choose. This helps give students practice with dexterity and speed so that they will have it when they do have a ball.

▶ Station 3, Partner Pass—Standing 10 feet (3 m) apart, partners pass the ball back and forth using chest or bounce passes.

▶ Station 4, Angle Pass—Standing 5 feet (1.5 m) from a wall, students pass the ball into the wall at a 45-degree angle, move to the side, make the catch, and pass back into the wall at a 45-degree angle.

▶ Station 5, Shuttle Run—Set cones approximately 25 feet (7.6 m) apart. On the go signal, students run from the start line to the opposite line, touch the line with their hand, and return to the start line.

▶ Station 6, Spot Shot—Set six spots in various locations around the key. Students begin shooting baskets from various spots. They cannot make two attempts in a row from the same spot.

▶ Station 7, Quick Dribble—Set cones approximately 15 feet (4.6 m) apart. On the go signal, students dribble from the starting cone to the opposite cone; after reaching the opposite cone, they turn and return to the starting cone.

▶ Station 8, Zigzag Dribble—Set up two lines of cones. The cones should be approximately 5 feet (1.5 m) apart and the lines approximately 8 feet (2.4 m) apart. Students begin at the first cone in the first line, dribble across to the first cone in the second line, turn and dribble to the second cone in the first line, and continue the zigzag pattern until all cones have been passed.

▶ Station 9, Push-Ups—Using their own modifications, students do as many push-ups as they can. This will help the students build the upper-body strength needed to pass and shoot quickly and accurately.

Name: _____ Date: _____

Basketball Skill Challenge Checklist

Beginning Level

Can You?

1. Alternate hands and dribble the ball 15 times under the left leg and 15 times under the right leg. ☐ Yes ☐ No

2. Standing with feet apart, complete a figure-8 dribble through and around the legs 15 times without a miss. ☐ Yes ☐ No

3. Bounce pass to your partner 15 feet (4.6 m) away 20 times. ☐ Yes ☐ No

4. Dribble the ball around your body five times in each direction. ☐ Yes ☐ No

5. While standing still, bounce the ball from behind through your legs and begin dribbling in front. Move the ball to the back and repeat five times with each hand. ☐ Yes ☐ No

6. Chest pass to your partner 10 feet (3 m) away 20 times. ☐ Yes ☐ No

7. While standing still, close your eyes and dribble the ball 15 times with each hand. ☐ Yes ☐ No

8. Standing with your feet apart, dribble the ball around and through your legs 10 times with each hand. ☐ Yes ☐ No

9. From a push-up position, dribble the ball under your body and back to the side for 45 seconds with each hand. ☐ Yes ☐ No

10. Dribble forward 20 feet (6 m) then backward to the starting line. Repeat this pattern five times with each hand. ☐ Yes ☐ No

I successfully completed all tasks: _____ Date:_____

Partner's initials: _____ Teacher's initials: _____

From Jeff Carpenter, 2007, *Physical Education Self-Management for Healthy, Active Lifestyles* (Champaign, IL: Human Kinetics).

Name: _____ Date: _____

Basketball Skill Challenge Checklist

Intermediate Level

Can You?

1. Pass the ball quickly around your body 15 times in both directions without a miss.   ☐ Yes   ☐ No

2. With your feet apart, hold the ball behind you, bounce the ball forward between your legs, and catch it eight times without a miss.   ☐ Yes   ☐ No

3. Repeat the skill above, but instead of catching the ball, begin dribbling when it passes between your legs.   ☐ Yes   ☐ No

4. Stand still, close your eyes, and dribble the ball 20 times with each hand without losing control.   ☐ Yes   ☐ No

5. Toss the ball in the air, sit down, and catch it.   ☐ Yes   ☐ No

6. Bounce the ball off the backboard, catch it, then make a shot. Do this five times.   ☐ Yes   ☐ No

7. Jog in place, pass the ball into the wall, and catch it eight times without stopping the jog.   ☐ Yes   ☐ No

I successfully completed all tasks: _____ Date: _____

Partner's initials: _____ Teacher's initials: _____

From Jeff Carpenter, 2007, *Physical Education Self-Management for Healthy, Active Lifestyles* (Champaign, IL: Human Kinetics).

CD-ROM

Name: _____ Date: _____

Basketball Skill Challenge Checklist

Advanced Level

Can You?

1. Sit in a chair and dribble the ball from the front to the back with each hand 10 times without losing control. ☐ Yes ☐ No

2. Hold the ball overhead, drop it, and catch it behind your back eight times without a miss. ☐ Yes ☐ No

3. With your feet apart, dribble a figure-8 pattern between and around your legs for 20 seconds. ☐ Yes ☐ No

4. Stand 15 feet (4.6 m) away from a partner, place a coin on the floor midway between you and your partner, and bounce pass a ball back and forth, hitting the coin 10 times. ☐ Yes ☐ No

5. Perform a crossover—from one hand to the other—dribble back and forth between your legs while moving forward for 30 seconds. ☐ Yes ☐ No

6. Standing 10 feet (3 m) from a wall, chest pass a ball into the wall while doing a shuffle step to the right 20 feet (6 m) and returning to the left. ☐ Yes ☐ No

7. Bounce the ball off the backboard, rebound it quickly, and shoot immediately. Repeat seven times and make five shots. ☐ Yes ☐ No

8. Beginning at the center line, dribble forward to the foul line, stop, and shoot. Repeat dribble and shoot five times. ☐ Yes ☐ No

9. From either end of the foul line, make three of five shots. ☐ Yes ☐ No

10. Make four of seven layups from the right side and four of seven from the left side. ☐ Yes ☐ No

I successfully completed all tasks: _____ Date: _____

Partner's initials: _____ Teacher's initials: _____

From Jeff Carpenter, 2007, *Physical Education Self-Management for Healthy, Active Lifestyles* (Champaign, IL: Human Kinetics).

Basketball
Station 1

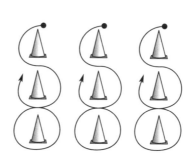

Cone
Dribble

Remember, change
hands as you pass
each cone.

From Jeff Carpenter, 2007, *Physical Education Self-Management for Healthy, Active Lifestyles* (Champaign, IL: Human Kinetics).

Basketball
Station 2

Jump
Rope

Try at least three
new steps.

From Jeff Carpenter, 2007, *Physical Education Self-Management for Healthy, Active Lifestyles* (Champaign, IL: Human Kinetics).

Basketball
Station 3

Partner
Pass

Remember, an accurate
pass is a good pass.

Basketball
Station 4

Angle
Pass

Use a side-shuffle to move
from side to side.

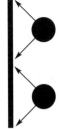

Basketball Station 5

Shuttle Run

When touching the line with your hand, remember to use the hand on the same side as the forward leg (when the right leg is forward, reach with the right hand).

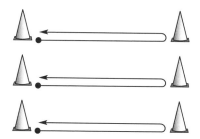

From Jeff Carpenter, 2007, *Physical Education Self-Management for Healthy, Active Lifestyles* (Champaign, IL: Human Kinetics).

Basketball Station 6

Spot Shot

Move quickly from one spot to another.

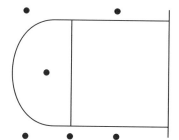

From Jeff Carpenter, 2007, *Physical Education Self-Management for Healthy, Active Lifestyles* (Champaign, IL: Human Kinetics).

CD-ROM

Basketball
Station 7

Quick
Dribble

Maintain control
by keeping the ball
below your waist.

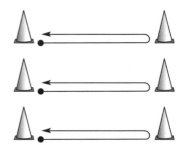

From Jeff Carpenter, 2007, *Physical Education Self-Management for Healthy, Active Lifestyles* (Champaign, IL: Human Kinetics).

Basketball
Station 8

Zigzag
Dribble

Change hands
at each cone.

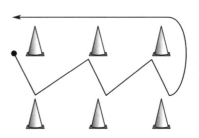

From Jeff Carpenter, 2007, *Physical Education Self-Management for Healthy, Active Lifestyles* (Champaign, IL: Human Kinetics).

Basketball
Station 9

Push-Ups

Use your own modification
(triceps with hands
in close, with hands
wide, on knees,
with one leg in the air).

From Jeff Carpenter, 2007, *Physical Education Self-Management for Healthy, Active Lifestyles* (Champaign, IL: Human Kinetics).

SOCCER SKILL CHALLENGES AND MOTIVATORS

Soccer provides an active team activity requiring a combination of physical skill, communication, and decision-making. With each skill challenge, students are able to practice one or more of these skills.

STANDARDS

▶ Physical Education Standard 1: Demonstrates competency in motor skills and movement patterns needed to perform a variety of physical activities.

▶ Physical Education Standard 2: Demonstrates understanding of movement concepts, principles, strategies, and tactics as they apply to the learning and performance of physical activities.

▶ Physical Education Standard 3: Participates regularly in physical activity.

▶ Health Education Standard 4: Students will demonstrate the ability to use interpersonal communication skills to enhance health and avoid or reduce health risks.

▶ Health Education Standard 7: Students will demonstrate the ability to practice health-enhancing behaviors and avoid or reduce health risks.

GET READY

▶ Set up one station for each skill challenge. If your facility does not have enough room for all the stations, set up as many as you can, taking one down and setting another up as students progress. On the first day of the challenge, set up stations only for the beginning level. As students begin to progress, provide stations for all levels.

▶ Each group of students should have one ball. If you do not have enough regulation soccer balls, substitute foam soccer balls, foam volleyballs, or 8.5-inch (21.6 cm) playground balls for dribbling and ball-control activities.

▶ Duplicate a skill challenge checklist for each student.

GET SET

▶ Demonstrate each of the challenge skills at the beginning level.

▶ Arrange students in pairs and distribute the equipment for each task. If you have an odd number of students, use groups of three with students rotating practice times.

◁ GO!

1. Ask all groups to begin practicing the skill for the beginning level of the first challenge. Not all students will successfully complete the challenges at the same time or at the same level.

2. As groups accomplish a challenge, they should check it off their skill challenge sheet and move to the next challenge. Spot check the sheets and give students appropriate feedback to keep them on track.

3. If students have difficulty accomplishing a task, have them demonstrate a lower-level skill, then break the new skill into small components, giving them time to practice each component. If, after practicing for a while, a student cannot meet the established goal but can meet part of it, note the accomplishment on the challenge sheet and let the student move on.

◁ STATIONS

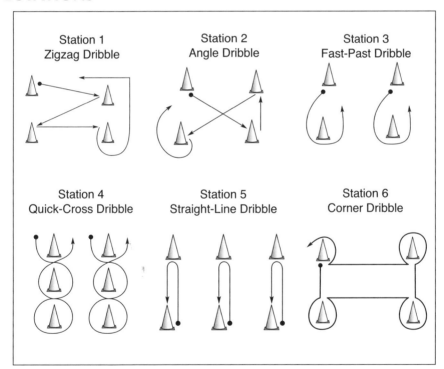

▶ Station 1, Zigzag Dribble— Place four cones in a square formation approximately 6 feet (1.8 m) apart. Place one ball by a cone. On the go signal, the player begins to dribble across the square to a cone, touches the cone, stops and traps the ball, touches the cone with their hand, dribbles across the square to another cone, touches the cone with their hand, dribbles to the third cone, dribbles behind the cone, and back to the starting point.

▶ Station 2, Angle Dribble— Place four cones in a square position approximately 10 feet (3 m) apart. Place one ball by a cone. On the go signal, the player begins to dribble across the center of the square to the opposite cone, touches the cone with their hand while continuing to dribble, moves to the cone at their left, touches that cone, dribbles across the center of the square to the opposite cone, touches the cone, and dribbles, to their right, back to the starting point.

▶ Station 3, Fast-Past Dribble— Place two cones approximately 6 feet (1.8 m) apart. Place one ball by a cone. On the go signal, the player begins to dribble as quickly as possible, while under control, to the opposite cone, goes around the cone, and dribbles back around the first cone. The player continues to dribble quickly around the cones for the entire time period.

▶ Station 4, Quick-Cross Dribble— Place three cones in a line approximately 4 feet (1.2 m) apart. Place a ball at one end cone. On the go signal, the player begins to dribble around the first cone, moves to the second, dribbles around that cone, moves to the last cone, and dribbles around it. After completing the sequence in one direction, the player reverses direction and repeats the sequence going back to the starting position.

▶ Station 5, Straight-Line Dribble— Place two cones in a straight line approximately 10 feet (3 m) apart. Place a ball by one cone. On the go signal, the player begins to dribble quickly to the next cone, touches the cone with their foot, turns, dribbles back to the first cone, touches it with their foot and repeats to sequence.

▶ Station 6, Corner Dribble— Place four cones in a rectangle formation approximately 6 feet (1.8 m) apart. Place a ball by one cone. On the go signal, the player begins to dribbles to the cone at their right, dribbles behind that cone, and repeats the sequence until all cones have been rounded. When returning to the first cone, the player turns, reverses directions, and repeats the sequence in the opposite direction.

Name: _____ Date: _____

Soccer Skill Challenge Checklist

Beginning Level

Can You?

1a. Standing in one place, kick with the instep to pass the ball to your partner who is 15 feet (4.6 m) away. Your partner should not have to move to trap the ball. Successfully pass the ball 10 times.   ☐ Yes   ☐ No

1b. Trap the ball passed from your partner with the sole of your foot. Successfully trap the ball 10 times.   ☐ Yes   ☐ No

2. Dribble the ball with alternating feet to a mark 25 feet (7.6 m) away and return while maintaining control.   ☐ Yes   ☐ No

3. Use an overhand throw-in to hit a hula hoop target 15 to 20 feet (4.6 to 6 m) away 7 out of 10 times.   ☐ Yes   ☐ No

4. Drop a ball from head height, let it bounce once, and trap it with your foot. Successfully trap it 10 times.   ☐ Yes   ☐ No

5. Standing, make 8 of 10 shots into the goal from a distance of 25 feet (7.6 m).   ☐ Yes   ☐ No

6. Punt a ball 20 feet (6 m) so that it passes through a pair of cones set 10 feet (3 m) apart.   ☐ Yes   ☐ No

7. Dribble the ball 15 feet (4.6 m), stop it on a line, and make 3 of 5 shots into the goal 20 feet (6 m) away.   ☐ Yes   ☐ No

8. Dribble the ball 15 feet (4.6 m), trap it, immediately turn 180 degrees, and dribble back to the start line. Perform 5 times in a row.   ☐ Yes   ☐ No

I successfully completed all tasks: _____ Date: _____

Partner's initials: _____ Teacher's initials: _____

From Jeff Carpenter, 2007, *Physical Education Self-Management for Healthy, Active Lifestyles* (Champaign, IL: Human Kinetics).

Name: _____ Date: _____

Soccer Skill Challenge Checklist

Intermediate Level

Can You?

1. Zigzag dribble down and back between four cones set 3 feet (1 m) apart while maintaining control. Perform three times in a row. □ Yes □ No

2. Dribble the ball 10 feet (3 m), trap it, and quickly kick it back to your partner. Your partner traps the ball, dribbles 10 feet (3 m) past you, and passes. Continue the length of the gym while maintaining control. □ Yes □ No

3. Knee dribble the ball three consecutive times. □ Yes □ No

4. As your partner tosses the ball toward you, trap it with your chest, pick it up, and toss it back to your partner. Perform five times. □ Yes □ No

5. Standing side by side with your partner who is 10 feet (3 m) away, pass the ball to each other while moving forward. Perform five consecutive passes. □ Yes □ No

6. Pass the ball to a wall 10 feet (3 m) away so that it comes directly back to you. Complete 10 consecutive passes. □ Yes □ No

7. Repeat challenge 6, but pass the ball at a 45-degree angle, move to the side, and trap the ball before passing it back at a 45-degree angle. Perform five times. □ Yes □ No

I successfully completed all tasks: _____ Date: _____

Partner's initials: _____ Teacher's initials: _____

From Jeff Carpenter, 2007, *Physical Education Self-Management for Healthy, Active Lifestyles* (Champaign, IL: Human Kinetics).

Name: _____ Date: _____

Soccer Skill Challenge Checklist

Advanced Level

Can You?

1. Zigzag dribble down and back between four cones, set 3 feet (1 m) apart, in less than 45 seconds. Repeat three times trying to beat your previous time.   ☐ Yes   ☐ No

2. Defend the goal from a partner's kick 7 out of 10 times.   ☐ Yes   ☐ No

3. Punt the ball 35 yards (32.2 m) so that it passes between two cones set 10 feet (3 m) apart 7 out of 10 times.   ☐ Yes   ☐ No

4. Bounce the ball off your knee, let it drop to the ground, dribble through three cones set 4 feet (1.2 m) apart, pick it up, and repeat on the way back. Complete three times.   ☐ Yes   ☐ No

5. Toss the ball in the air, head it, let it drop to the ground, and trap it. Complete four times.   ☐ Yes   ☐ No

6. Toss the ball in the air, head it, knee it, and then catch it 7 out of 10 times.   ☐ Yes   ☐ No

7. With you and a partner in a 15 × 15 foot (4.6 × 4.6 m) area, try to take the ball away from your partner within 10 seconds. Switch and let your partner attempt a steal. Successfully steal the ball five times.   ☐ Yes   ☐ No

8. While running beside your partner, try to steal the ball. Once you have control, begin to dribble and let your partner try to steal it from you. Keep within a 12-foot (3.6 m) lane. Successfully steal the ball five times.   ☐ Yes   ☐ No

I successfully completed all tasks: _____ Date:_____

Partner's initials: _____ Teacher's initials: _____

From Jeff Carpenter, 2007, *Physical Education Self-Management for Healthy, Active Lifestyles* (Champaign, IL: Human Kinetics).

Soccer Station 1

Zigzag Dribble

Zigzag dribble through the cones as quickly as possible.

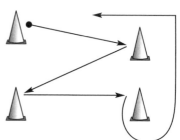

Soccer Station 2

Angle Dribble

Begin at one side, dribble to the opposite side, and continue the pattern.

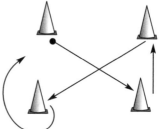

Soccer Station 3

Fast-Past Dribble

Dribble down, circle
the end cone,
and quickly dribble back.

From Jeff Carpenter, 2007, *Physical Education Self-Management for Healthy, Active Lifestyles* (Champaign, IL: Human Kinetics).

✂ -

Soccer Station 4

Quick-Cross Dribble

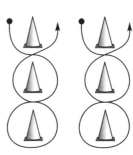

Begin at one side,
dribble to the opposite side,
and continue the pattern.

From Jeff Carpenter, 2007, *Physical Education Self-Management for Healthy, Active Lifestyles* (Champaign, IL: Human Kinetics).

Soccer Station 5

Straight-Line Dribble

Moving as quickly as possible, dribble the ball between the cones.

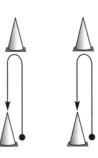

From Jeff Carpenter, 2007, *Physical Education Self-Management for Healthy, Active Lifestyles* (Champaign, IL: Human Kinetics).

✂ -

Soccer Station 6

Corner Dribble

Dribble around the square, circling each cone before moving on.

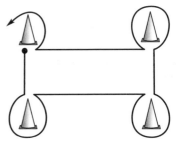

From Jeff Carpenter, 2007, *Physical Education Self-Management for Healthy, Active Lifestyles* (Champaign, IL: Human Kinetics).

SOFTBALL SKILL CHALLENGES AND MOTIVATORS

Softball has become a true lifetime activity. From school and community teams for young children and adolescents to senior citizens, softball provides an enjoyable physical activity.

⬛ STANDARDS

▶ Physical Education Standard 1: Demonstrates competency in motor skills and movement patterns needed to perform a variety of physical activities.

▶ Physical Education Standard 2: Demonstrates understanding of movement concepts, principles, strategies, and tactics as they apply to the learning and performance of physical activities.

▶ Physical Education Standard 3: Participates regularly in physical activity.

▶ Health Education Standard 4: Students will demonstrate the ability to use interpersonal communication skills to enhance health and avoid or reduce health risks.

▶ Health Education Standard 7: Students will demonstrate the ability to practice health-enhancing behaviors and avoid or reduce health risks.

⬛ GET READY

▶ Using bases or cones, set up enough softball diamonds to accommodate the class when divided into groups of six.

▶ Duplicate a skill challenge checklist for each student.

⬛ GET SET

▶ Demonstrate each of the challenge skills at the beginning level.

▶ Place one group at each diamond, with students playing the six infield positions, including pitcher and catcher.

⬛ GO!

Ask all groups to begin practicing the skill for the beginning level of the first challenge. Not all students will successfully complete the challenges at the same time or at the same level. After 3 minutes, players rotate positions. Players repeat the same task for the 3 minutes they play each position. As groups accomplish a challenge, they should check it off their skill challenge sheet and move to the next challenge. Spot check the sheets and give students appropriate feedback to keep them on track. If students have difficulty accomplishing a task, have them demonstrate a lower-level skill, then break the new skill into small components, giving them time to practice each. If, after practicing for a while, a student cannot meet the established goal but can meet part of it, note the accomplishment on the challenge sheet and let the student move on.

STATIONS

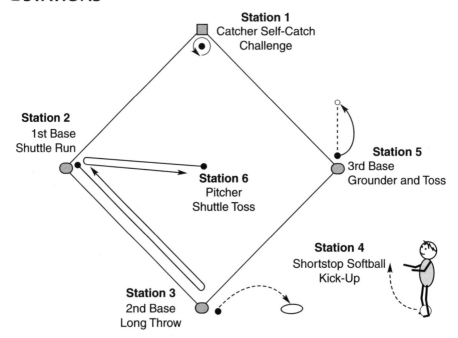

- ▶ Station 1, Catcher Self-Catch Challenge—Place one softball at home plate. On the go signal, the player picks up the ball and begins the challenge. First tossing the ball in the air, approximately 5 feet, and catching it. If successful, try the following modifications—toss, clap 3 times, and catch; toss, turn a half circle, and catch; toss, turn a full circle, and catch; toss, sit down, and catch; or toss, lie down, and catch.

- ▶ Station 2, 1st Base Shuttle Run—On the go signal, the player standing at 1st base runs to 2nd base, touches the base, and returns. This sequence is repeated for the entire time period.

- ▶ Station 3, 2nd Base Long Throw—Place four softballs on 2nd base and a hula-hoop target on the ground approximately 20 feet (6 m) away. On the go signal, the player attempts to toss the ball from 2nd base, landing in the hoop. The player attempts the toss with all four balls before running to pick up the balls and returning to 2nd base to make additional attempts.

▶ Station 4, Shortstop Softball Kick-Up—Place one ball at the shortstop position. On the go signal, the player places the ball between their feet, jumps in the air, releases the ball by bringing both feet upward, and attempts to catch the ball.

▶ Station 5, 3rd Base Grounder and Toss—Place one ball at 3rd base. On the go signal, the player rolls the ball forward, counts to 3, and runs in front of the ball and catches it before the ball stops rolling. After picking the ball up, the player runs back to 3rd base and rolls the ball again.

▶ Station 6, Pitcher's Toss-Up—Place one ball on the pitcher's mound. On the go signal, the pitcher picks up the ball, tosses it approximately 6 feet (1.8 m) in the air, catches it, and runs to 1st base. After touching 1st base, the pitcher again tosses the ball in the air, catches it, and returns to the pitcher's mound. The sequence is repeated for the entire time period.

Name: _____ Date: _____

Softball Skill Challenge Checklist

Beginning Level

Can You?

1. Toss a ball straight up and catch it 18 out of 20 tries. ☐ Yes ☐ No

2. From a standing position, toss a ball straight up, touch the floor with your hands, then catch the ball 12 out of 15 tries. ☐ Yes ☐ No

3. Toss a ball straight up, sit down, and catch it 7 out of 10 tries. ☐ Yes ☐ No

4. Run from first base to second base and back (bases are 30 feet [9 m] apart) in 20 seconds. ☐ Yes ☐ No

5. Place a softball between your feet, kick it up, and catch it three out of five times. ☐ Yes ☐ No

6. Stand on the floor next to a partner who is standing on a bench, holding a ball at his or her head height. As he or she drops the ball, catch it 7 of 10 times. Complete five times. ☐ Yes ☐ No

7. With a partner standing on a bench or chair facing you, hit the ball when he or she drops it. Hit the ball 5 of 10 times. ☐ Yes ☐ No

8. Catch a grounder and immediately throw it to a target 30 feet (9 m) away. Hit the target 7 of 10 times. ☐ Yes ☐ No

9. While your partner is standing 10 feet (3 m) away from you, he or she tosses the ball into the air. Run and catch it before the ball hits the ground. Catch it 7 of 10 times. ☐ Yes ☐ No

I successfully completed all tasks: _____ Date: _____

Partner's initials: _____ Teacher's initials: _____

Name: _____ Date: _____

Softball Skill Challenge Checklist

Intermediate Level

Can You?

1. Throw a ball overhand to your partner 35 feet (10.5 m) away so that
   he or she can catch it without moving 17 out of 20 times.   ☐ Yes   ☐ No

2. Catch a throw from your partner 35 feet (10.5 m) away 17 out of 20 times.   ☐ Yes   ☐ No

3. Pitch underhand and hit a hula hoop target taped on a wall 30 feet (9 m)
   away 8 out of 10 times.   ☐ Yes   ☐ No

4. Hit 6 out of 10 pitched balls (pitched within the strike zone).   ☐ Yes   ☐ No

5. Hit 6 out of 10 self-tossed balls.   ☐ Yes   ☐ No

6. Play pickle with two partners and successfully tag the runner out 7 out of
   10 times. (Pickle is a game in which two players are each on a base
   and another player is between them on the baseline. The player between
   the bases tries to reach a base before being tagged with the ball. Base
   players toss the ball back and forth and can run toward the runner.)   ☐ Yes   ☐ No

7. Standing 15 feet (4.6 m) from a wall, throw a tennis ball at the wall,
   catch it, and throw it back 15 times in 30 seconds.   ☐ Yes   ☐ No

8. Toss a ball into the air, turn in a complete circle, and catch the ball
   8 out of 10 times.   ☐ Yes   ☐ No

I successfully completed all tasks: _____ Date:_____

Partner's initials: _____ Teacher's initials: _____

Name: _____ Date: _____

Softball Skill Challenge Checklist

Advanced Level

Can You?

1. Facing a wall, throw a tennis ball at the wall, turn, and catch it over your shoulder 7 out of 10 times.   ☐ Yes   ☐ No

2. Play short hop with your partner and catch the ball 7 out of 10 times. (To play short hop, one partner tosses the ball so that it bounces off the floor about 2 feet [0.6 m] in front of the other partner.)   ☐ Yes   ☐ No

3. While your partner is standing 20 feet (6 m) away tossing you a ball, catch it with your nondominant hand 17 out of 20 times.   ☐ Yes   ☐ No

4. Play pickle with two other people and successfully reach a base two out of five times.   ☐ Yes   ☐ No

5. With your partner kneeling and swinging a Wiffle ball tied to a long cord over his or her head, hit the ball with a bat 7 out of 10 times.   ☐ Yes   ☐ No

6. Bunt a tossed ball to target cones placed to your left, right, and directly in front of you. Hit each target four times.   ☐ Yes   ☐ No

7. Toss a ball underhand into a bucket suspended between two posts 7 out of 10 times.   ☐ Yes   ☐ No

8. Throw a ball through a hula hoop target suspended between two posts 30 feet (9 m) away 8 out of 10 times.   ☐ Yes   ☐ No

I successfully completed all tasks: _____ Date:_____

Partner's initials: _____ Teacher's initials: _____

From Jeff Carpenter, 2007, *Physical Education Self-Management for Healthy, Active Lifestyles* (Champaign, IL: Human Kinetics).

Name: _____ Date: _____

Softball Station Motivator

Catcher Self-Catch Challenge

Toss the ball into the air, turn 180 degrees, clap hands, and catch the ball.

First Base Shuttle Run

Beginning at first base, run to second base and return as quickly as possible. Repeat.

Second Base Long Throw

Toss balls into a hula hoop target lying on the ground 20 feet (6 m) away.

Station 1
Catcher Self-Catch
Challenge

Station 2
1st Base
Shuttle Run

Station 6
Pitcher
Shuttle Toss

Station 5
3rd Base
Grounder and Toss

Station 4
Shortstop Softball
Kick-Up

Station 3
2nd Base
Long Throw

Shortstop Softball Kick-Up

Put a softball between your feet. Jump and kick the ball into the air and catch it.

Third Base Grounder and Toss

Roll a ball on the ground, count to three, then run in front of the ball and catch it. Repeat.

Pitcher Shuttle Toss

Toss the ball into the air and catch it, run to first base, repeat the toss and catch, and run back to the pitcher's area.

From Jeff Carpenter, 2007, *Physical Education Self-Management for Healthy, Active Lifestyles* (Champaign, IL: Human Kinetics).

VOLLEYBALL SKILL CHALLENGES AND MOTIVATORS

Volleyball requires both individual and team skills. Like other team activities, skill, communication, and cooperation are involved. While volleyball skills can be difficult for some, using selected modifications in court size, net height, and type of ball (regulation or large trainers) increase individual motivation through successful experiences.

STANDARDS

▶ Physical Education Standard 1: Demonstrates competency in motor skills and movement patterns needed to perform a variety of physical activities.

▶ Physical Education Standard 2: Demonstrates understanding of movement concepts, principles, strategies, and tactics as they apply to the learning and performance of physical activities.

▶ Physical Education Standard 3: Participates regularly in physical activity.

▶ Health Education Standard 4: Students will demonstrate the ability to use interpersonal communication skills to enhance health and avoid or reduce health risks.

▶ Health Education Standard 7: Students will demonstrate the ability to practice health-enhancing behaviors and avoid or reduce health risks.

GET READY

▶ Arrange stations so that students can move around and be successful within designated areas without interference from other stations.

▶ To allow for maximum success, use volleyball trainers and low nets where and when appropriate. For younger and less-experienced students use a volleyball trainer, beach ball, or balloon rather than a regulation volleyball.

▶ Place one set of dice at each station.

▶ When using a net or a line on the wall, lower the height to approximately the level an average person in the class can reach up and touch.

▶ Move the service line closer to the net if that will help students be successful; the distance will vary from 3 to 5 feet (1 to 1.5 m) depending on the ability of the students.

▶ When students are hitting against a wall, the wall line should be the same height as the net students are using. Remind students to stand 2 to 3 feet (0.6 to 1 m) from the wall in order to make consistent and successful hits.

▶ Duplicate a skill challenge checklist for each student.

GET SET

▷ Demonstrate each of the challenge skills at the beginning level.

▷ Arrange students in pairs and distribute the equipment for each task. If you have an odd number of students, use groups of three with students rotating practice times.

▷ Each student will roll the dice at the stations to determine the number of repetitions to complete.

GO!

1. Ask all groups to begin practicing the skill for the beginning level of the first challenge. Not all students will successfully complete the challenges at the same time or at the same level.

2. As groups accomplish a challenge, they should check it off their skill challenge sheet and move to the next challenge. Spot check the sheets and give students appropriate feedback to keep them on track.

3. If students have difficulty accomplishing a task, have them demonstrate a lower-level skill, then break the new skill into small components, giving them time to practice each. If, after practicing for a while, a student cannot meet the established goal but can meet part of it, note the accomplishment on the challenge sheet and let the student move on.

STATIONS

▷ Station 1, Overhead Volley—Place a taped line approximately 8 feet (2.4 m) up on a wall (for less skilled players the line may be lower). Place another line approximately 5 feet (1.5 m) from the wall. Place one volleyball or trainer on the line. On the go signal, the player picks up the ball, tosses it in the air, and sets or bumps it into the wall above the line. As the ball rebounds off the wall, the player attempts to hit the ball back without catching it.

▷ Station 2, Serving—Without using a net, place a hula-hoop approximately 15 feet (4.6 m) from a "serving" line. Place three volleyballs or trainers on the "serving" line. On the go signal, the player picks up the ball and, using either an overhand or underhand motion, attempts to serve the ball into the hoop. After three attempts the player runs down, picks up the balls, returns to the "serving" line, and repeats the sequence.

▷ Station 3, Net Recoveries—Place a well-tensioned net in an open area. Place one volleyball or trainer by the net. On the go signal, the player picks up the ball and tosses it into the net. On the rebound, the player bumps the ball straight up, catches it, and repeats the sequence.

▷ Station 4, Bumping—Place a taped line approximately 5 feet (1.5 m) up on a wall and a start line 5 feet (1.5 m) from the wall. Place one volleyball or trainer by the wall. On the go signal, the player tosses the

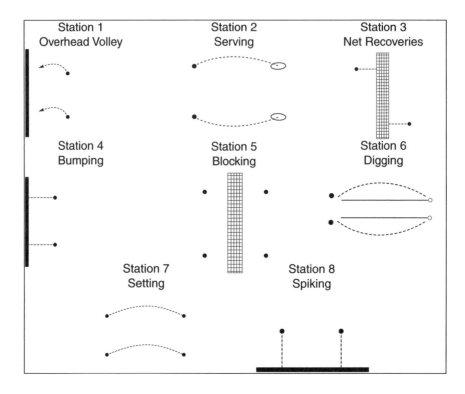

ball into the wall, above the line. On the rebound, they bump the ball back against the wall without catching it. The player continues to bump the ball without catching it. If the ball hits the ground, the player picks it up and begins the sequence again.

▶ Station 5, Blocking—Standing with partners on opposite sides of a net, give a volleyball or trainer to one player. On the go signal, the player with the ball tosses it up and over the net. As the ball begins to go over the net, the partner jumps straight into the air with both hands up and blocks the ball. After four tosses, players switch roles.

▶ Station 6, Digging—With partners standing 6-8 feet (1.8-2.4 m) apart, one player tosses a ball to their partner—the toss should reach the partner below their waist—and the receiving partner "digs" the ball, hitting it back to their partner. After four tosses, players switch roles.

▶ Station 7, Setting—With partners standing approximately 10 feet (3 m) apart, one player tosses the ball high in the air to their partner. Receiving the toss, the ball is set back to the "tossing" partner who returns the ball with an overhead set. The rotation continues until the ball touches the ground.

▶ Station 8, Spiking—Place one volleyball or trainer on a line 6 feet (1.8 m) from a wall. On the go signal, the player picks up the ball, tosses it in the air, jumps and "spikes" the ball, with an open hand, down against the wall.

Name: _____ Date: _____

Volleyball Skill Challenge Checklist

Beginning Level

Can You?

1. Volley a ball back to your partner 8 out of 10 times when he or she
   tosses it to you.   ☐ Yes   ☐ No

2. Volley a ball above an 8-foot (2.4 m) line on the wall 10 times while
   maintaining control of the ball and standing 5 feet (1.5 m) from the wall.   ☐ Yes   ☐ No

3. Volley a ball, at least 4 feet (1.2 m) above your head, to yourself
   for 20 seconds while maintaining control of the ball.   ☐ Yes   ☐ No

4. From the service line for your age group, use an underhand serve
   to hit into the receiving court 8 out of 10 times.   ☐ Yes   ☐ No

5. Dig a ball tossed by your partner below your waist 8 out of 10 times.   ☐ Yes   ☐ No

6. Bump a ball above an 8-foot (2.4 m) line on the wall 10 times while
   maintaining control of the ball and standing 5 feet (1.5 m) from the wall.   ☐ Yes   ☐ No

7. Without using a net, toss the ball into the air, jump up, and spike it
   8 out of 10 times.   ☐ Yes   ☐ No

8. Volley the ball back and forth with your partner five times while
   maintaining control of the ball.   ☐ Yes   ☐ No

I successfully completed all tasks: _____ Date:_____

Partner's initials: _____ Teacher's initials: _____

From Jeff Carpenter, 2007, *Physical Education Self-Management for Healthy, Active Lifestyles* (Champaign, IL: Human Kinetics).

Name: _____ Date: _____

Volleyball Skill Challenge Checklist

Intermediate Level

Can You?

1. Volley the ball at least 4 feet (1.2 m) above your head 10 times while standing in a hula hoop and maintaining control of the ball. ☐ Yes ☐ No

2. Set or bump the ball above your head, turn 90 degrees, and set or bump the ball again. Complete eight times. ☐ Yes ☐ No

3. Toss the ball into the air and successfully set it to your partner 8 out of 10 times. ☐ Yes ☐ No

4. Complete 8 out of 10 overhand serves—from the service line appropriate for your age—into the receiving court. ☐ Yes ☐ No

5. Set or bump the ball above your head, turn 180 degrees, and set or bump the ball again. Complete five times. ☐ Yes ☐ No

6. Bump a ball against the wall (above an 8-foot [2.4 m] line) for 15 seconds. ☐ Yes ☐ No

7. Standing by a net, toss the ball into the air and set it to your partner so that the ball is within 1 foot (0.3 m) of the net 8 out of 10 times. ☐ Yes ☐ No

8. Using a 5- or 6-foot (1.5 or 1.8 m) net, spike a ball tossed by your partner over the net 8 out of 10 times. ☐ Yes ☐ No

I successfully completed all tasks: _____ Date:_____

Partner's initials: _____ Teacher's initials: _____

From Jeff Carpenter, 2007, *Physical Education Self-Management for Healthy, Active Lifestyles* (Champaign, IL: Human Kinetics).

Name: _____ Date: _____

Volleyball Skill Challenge Checklist

Advanced Level

Can You?

1. Toss the ball overhead, set it, let it bounce on the floor, and then dig it. Successfully complete the sequence 10 times. ☐ Yes ☐ No

2. Set or bump the ball, turn 360 degrees, and then set or bump the ball again. Successfully complete the sequence 10 times without the ball touching the ground or being caught. ☐ Yes ☐ No

3. Spike a ball set by your partner over the net 8 out of 10 times. ☐ Yes ☐ No

4. Using an overhand serve, serve 10 out of 10 times into the receiving court. ☐ Yes ☐ No

5. Using either an underhand or overhand serve, hit the ball into each quadrant of the receiving court. Successfully complete the sequence five times. ☐ Yes ☐ No

6. From the backcourt, successfully toss the ball up and set it to your partner, who is standing close to the net, 8 out of 10 times. ☐ Yes ☐ No

7. Toss the ball up and back set it to your partner 8 out of 10 times. Your partner is standing 5 feet (1.5 m) behind you. ☐ Yes ☐ No

8. With your partner, successfully volley the ball back and forth for 30 seconds while maintaining control. ☐ Yes ☐ No

I successfully completed all tasks: _____ Date:_____

Partner's initials: _____ Teacher's initials: _____

From Jeff Carpenter, 2007, *Physical Education Self-Management for Healthy, Active Lifestyles* (Champaign, IL: Human Kinetics).

Volleyball Station 1

Overhead Volley

Standing 5 feet (1.5 m) away, volley the ball over an 8-foot (2.4 m) line taped to the wall.

From Jeff Carpenter, 2007, *Physical Education Self-Management for Healthy, Active Lifestyles* (Champaign, IL: Human Kinetics).

Volleyball Station 2

Serving

Serve, underhand or overhand, into the targets.

From Jeff Carpenter, 2007, *Physical Education Self-Management for Healthy, Active Lifestyles* (Champaign, IL: Human Kinetics).

CD-ROM

Volleyball Station 3

Net Recoveries

Toss the ball into the net and bump the rebound straight up.

From Jeff Carpenter, 2007, *Physical Education Self-Management for Healthy, Active Lifestyles* (Champaign, IL: Human Kinetics).

Volleyball Station 4

Blocking

Block your partner's throw across the net.

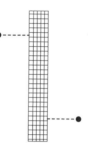

From Jeff Carpenter, 2007, *Physical Education Self-Management for Healthy, Active Lifestyles* (Champaign, IL: Human Kinetics).

Volleyball Station 5

Bumping

Standing 5 feet (1.5 m) away from the wall, bump the ball against it.

From Jeff Carpenter, 2007, *Physical Education Self-Management for Healthy, Active Lifestyles* (Champaign, IL: Human Kinetics).

Volleyball Station 6

Digging

Dig the ball your partner has tossed low.

From Jeff Carpenter, 2007, *Physical Education Self-Management for Healthy, Active Lifestyles* (Champaign, IL: Human Kinetics).

Volleyball
Station 7

Setting

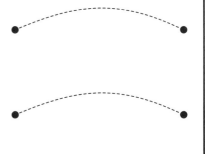

Standing 10 feet (3 m)
away from your partner,
volley the ball back and forth.

Volleyball
Station 8

Spiking

Toss the ball in the air,
jump up, and spike it down
against the wall. Can you
dig the rebound?

Group Activities and Challenges

The first activities were presented in the form of individual and partner challenges and motivators. The class format was based on using stations with students moving through the progression at their own pace, practicing skills until they were successful. Although this format has proven successful for the activities presented, other activities are best presented using small-group and partner formats.

The following activities are presented in a group format. However, they still allow for individual pacing, challenges, and goal setting.

Golf Challenges

Golf is one of the lifelong activities physical educators teach: Instruction can begin at about age 4 and continue throughout life. And people around the world enjoy participating in golf regardless of their ability. When teaching intermediate grades and middle school level students basic golf knowledge and skills, teachers introduce students to an activity that can provide a physical and mental challenge along with physical activity for a lifetime.

Before beginning instruction and practice in golf, you must address safety procedures. Designate a waiting or stay-clear zone in the instructional and practice area by placing caution tape or another physical barrier between this area and the swinging area. Also instruct students to always look before moving and to always look to make sure the area is clear before swinging a club. Before presenting the following challenge activities, be sure to provide appropriate instruction related to grip, alignment, swing technique, and so on.

PUTTING: THE FIRST STEP TO SUCCESS IN GOLF

Putting is the key to success in golf. Many golfers can drive well and hit great fairway shots, but without sound putting skills they are not able to achieve the goal of having a low score. Putting can be practiced in the gym, on a carpet, on a mat, or on short grass, and it can be used to teach the fundamentals of grip, stance, take-away, and follow-through. It is truly the first step to success in golf.

◢ STANDARDS

▶ Physical Education Standard 1: Demonstrates competency in motor skills and movement patterns needed to perform a variety of physical activities.

▶ Physical Education Standard 2: Demonstrates understanding of movement concepts, principles, strategies, and tactics as they apply to the learning and performance of physical activities.

▶ Physical Education Standard 5: Exhibits responsible personal and social behavior that respects self and others in physical activity settings.

◢ GET READY

▶ Prepare a challenge card for each student.

▶ Set up five stations around the facility. Each station will include four putting sites. Include the following:

- Carpet strips approximately 15 × 3 inches (38 × 7.6 cm)
- Two folding mats
- Three balls and one putter at each putting site.

◢ GET SET

At each station demonstrate the challenge and review proper form: using a pendulum swing with the shoulders and keeping the hands and wrists solid through the motion. Also remind students that it is not only how hard they stroke the ball but also the accuracy directed by the backstroke and follow-through.

◢ GO!

1. Assign students to the stations. Groups of six to eight at each station with partners at each site within the station works best.

2. One student stands at the start line and his or her partner stands by the target. As one partner strokes the ball, the other partner picks it up after it has stopped. After the attempts, they switch positions. The rotation continues for approximately 7 minutes before the groups rotate among stations.

3. Students keep track of their attempts and successes on their challenge cards. After all the groups have been to all the stations, each group totals their successful attempts to see if group and individual goals were accomplished.

4. After the first day of this activity, place the cards in a folder and bring them out the next time to see if students can better their first score.

◁ STATIONS

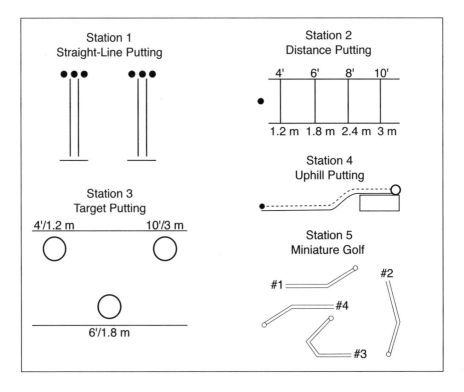

▶ Station 1, Straight-Line Putting—Tape a lane 8 feet × 4 inches (2.4 m × 10 cm) on the floor or carpet strip. Place three balls at one end of the lane. Each student putts three balls per turn, attempting to putt the ball slightly past the other end and keeping the ball within the 4-inch (10 cm) lane.

▶ Station 2, Distance Putting—On the floor or carpet strips, place lines at 4 feet, 6 feet, 8 feet, and 10 feet (1.2, 1.8, 2.4, and 3 m). Each partner attempts to putt and place balls first on the 4-foot (1.2 m) line, followed by the 6-foot (1.8 m) line, the 8-foot (2.4 m) line, and then the 10-foot (3 m) line.

▶ Station 3, Target Putting—Tape paper cups, lying on their side, approximately 4 feet, 6 feet, and 10 feet (1.2, 1.8, and 3 m) from the start line. Students attempt to putt the ball into any of the cups.

▶ Station 4, Uphill Putting—Place a folding mat under the carpet strip, unfolding two sections and leaving two sections folded. Tape a large paper cup, lying on its side, at the top of the folded section. Students attempt to putt the ball up the incline into the cup.

▶ Station 5, Miniature Golf—Using carpet strips or lines on the floor, design a four-hole course. Place cones along the course as obstacles and tape a paper cup, lying on its side, at the end. Have students keep their score—one stroke or point for each time they hit the ball. If a ball goes off the carpet strip or outside the lines, it is considered out of bounds and a stroke is added to the student's score to bring it back inbounds (but no closer to the hole). At the end of the course, students should add up their total score.

Name: _____ Date: _____

Putt-for-the-Gold Challenge

	Attempts	Successes
Straight-Line Putting		
Distance Putting		
Target Putting		
Uphill Putting		
Miniature Golf		
Total successes		

From Jeff Carpenter, 2007, *Physical Education Self-Management for Healthy, Active Lifestyles* (Champaign, IL: Human Kinetics).

Putt-for-the-Gold
Station 1

Straight-Line Putting

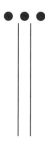

Remember to follow through
and keep your putter square
to the end of the lane.

From Jeff Carpenter, 2007, *Physical Education Self-Management for Healthy, Active Lifestyles* (Champaign, IL: Human Kinetics).

Putt-for-the-Gold
Station 2

Distance Putting

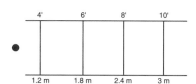

Remember to use
your arms, not your wrists.

From Jeff Carpenter, 2007, *Physical Education Self-Management for Healthy, Active Lifestyles* (Champaign, IL: Human Kinetics).

Putt-for-the-Gold
Station 3

Target
Putting

Remember, keep your
head and body still.

4'/1.2 m   10'/3 m
○   ○

○
6'/1.8 m

From Jeff Carpenter, 2007, *Physical Education Self-Management for Healthy, Active Lifestyles* (Champaign, IL: Human Kinetics).

✂ -

Putt-for-the-Gold
Station 4

Uphill
Putting

Remember to look at the
green and see if it slopes
downhill after the cup.

From Jeff Carpenter, 2007, *Physical Education Self-Management for Healthy, Active Lifestyles* (Champaign, IL: Human Kinetics).

Putt-for-the-Gold
Station 5

Miniature Golf

Remember to take the challenges in stride and have fun.

From Jeff Carpenter, 2007, *Physical Education Self-Management for Healthy, Active Lifestyles* (Champaign, IL: Human Kinetics).

CHIPPING: GETTING INTO THE GOLF SWING

Review the basic elements of the golf swing: The stance is square to the target, feet are shoulder-width apart, knees are slightly bent, head is still with eyes down, wrists are firm, and the hips and arms move as a unit. Remind students that there is little difference between chipping and a full swing except that when chipping, the swing is limited to bringing the club back parallel to the ground and has a short follow-through. The weight transfers slightly to the rear foot and shifts forward as the club moves forward.

STANDARDS

▶ Physical Education Standard 1: Demonstrates competency in motor skills and movement patterns needed to perform a variety of physical activities.

▶ Physical Education Standard 2: Demonstrates understanding of movement concepts, principles, strategies, and tactics as they apply to the learning and performance of physical activities.

▶ Physical Education Standard 5: Exhibits responsible personal and social behavior that respects self and others in physical activity settings.

GET READY

▶ As students begin to take longer swings, review all safety procedures frequently throughout the lesson.

▶ When preparing a practice area, consider the format for a basic chipping practice area in the floor diagram.

▶ Prepare a challenge card for each student.

Target area	Target area	Target area	Target area
Hitting area (1 person only)	Hitting area (1 person only)	Hitting area (1 person only)	Hitting area (1 person only)
Line formed with tape or by a series of cones			
Waiting area	Waiting area	Waiting area	Waiting area

GET SET

► Arrange a safe hitting area for the appropriate challenge.

► Depending on the abilities of individual students and the class, the type of ball used may vary: regulation golf ball, practice golf ball, wiffle ball (baseball or softball size), or tennis ball.

► Assign two or three students per practice area. Remind them that students who are waiting must stay in the waiting area and students who are hitting must stay in the hitting area until all students have completed their attempts and the signal to retrieve the balls is given.

► After a student has completed three attempts, he or she lays down the club and waits for the signal.

GO!

1. Explain the challenge and how to record attempts and successes on individual cards.

2. On the go signal, all students in the hitting zone begin. After their three attempts, clubs are put down.

3. On the next signal, balls are retrieved and brought back to the hitting area.

4. On another signal, students rotate. When they are all safely in position, the next go signal is given.

5. Students in the waiting area complete their challenge card.

STATIONS

► Station 1, Tennis Chip—Students attempt to chip a tennis ball into the target zone directly in front of their hitting area. If the ball bounces out, count it as a success.

► Station 2, Target Chip—Place a large hula hoop in the target zone. Students attempt to hit the golf ball into the hoop. If the ball bounces or rolls in or hits in and bounces out, count it as a success.

► Station 3, Distance Chip—Extend the target area by approximately 20 yards (18 m). Place lines 5, 10, 15, and 20 yards (4.6, 9, 13.7, and 18 m) from the hitting zone. Jump ropes work well. The student attempts to chip the ball into the closest area, then into the middle area, and finally the farthest area. One point is given for each successful chip.

► Station 4, Angle Chip—Using the hitting grid, have students attempt to chip the ball to the right or left into another group's hitting zone.

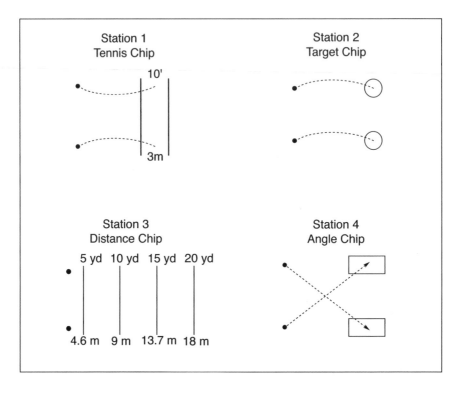

Station 1
Tennis Chip

Station 2
Target Chip

Station 3
Distance Chip

Station 4
Angle Chip

Teacher Note

Using the same teaching and practice format (i.e., a safe hitting area), have the students begin developing a fuller swing, but a maximum of a three-quarter swing. (It is not necessary to present a full swing when focusing on technique and basic skill, and it can detract from using appropriate technique and control.) The maximum length to a target should be approximately 50 yards (45 m).

Name: _____ Date: _____

Chip Away Challenge

	Attempts	Successes
Tennis Chip		
Target Chip		
Distance Chip		
Angle Chip		
Total successes		

From Jeff Carpenter, 2007, *Physical Education Self-Management for Healthy, Active Lifestyles* (Champaign, IL: Human Kinetics).

Chip Away Challenge
Station 1

Tennis
Chip

10'

3 m

Using a tennis ball, chip the ball from the starting area into the target zone. Even if it bounces and lands in the zone, it counts. (Hint: Remember, shorten your swing depending on the distance to the target.)

From Jeff Carpenter, 2007, *Physical Education Self-Management for Healthy, Active Lifestyles* (Champaign, IL: Human Kinetics).

Chip Away Challenge
Station 2

Target Chip

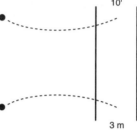

This challenge is the same as Tennis Chip, only this time you are using a golf ball. (Hint: Remember, shorten your swing depending on the distance to the target. Also, if the ball hits short of the target and rolls or bounces in, it still counts.)

From Jeff Carpenter, 2007, *Physical Education Self-Management for Healthy, Active Lifestyles* (Champaign, IL: Human Kinetics).

CD-ROM

Chip Away Challenge Station 3

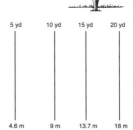

Distance Chip

There are four target areas, each 5 yards apart. The first is 5 yards away, followed by areas at 10, 15, and 20 yards from the start line. Chip your first ball into the first area, followed with the next ball into the second area, and so on. Record one point for each area your ball lands in.

From Jeff Carpenter, 2007, *Physical Education Self-Management for Healthy, Active Lifestyles* (Champaign, IL: Human Kinetics).

Chip Away Challenge Station 4

Angle Chip

Standing in your section of the hitting area, chip a ball into the target area of all the other sections of the hitting area. (Hint: Remember to set your stance and club face toward each target area and to adjust your swing depending on the distance to the target.)

From Jeff Carpenter, 2007, *Physical Education Self-Management for Healthy, Active Lifestyles* (Champaign, IL: Human Kinetics).

CHIP-AND-PUTT GROUP GOLF CHALLENGE

This is a fun and challenging activity that lets students use their creativity in designing a chip-and-putt course while practicing their skills. Additionally, students work in cooperation in small groups during the design and practice phases.

STANDARDS

▶ Physical Education Standard 1: Demonstrates competency in motor skills and movement patterns needed to perform a variety of physical activities.

▶ Physical Education Standard 2: Demonstrates understanding of movement concepts, principles, strategies, and tactics as they apply to the learning and performance of physical activities.

▶ Physical Education Standard 5: Exhibits responsible personal and social behavior that respects self and others in physical activity settings.

GET READY

▶ This activity is best done outside.

▶ Make available putting carpets, cones, hula hoops, paper or plastic cups, tape, golf or tennis balls, putters, wedges, and 9 and 8 irons.

▶ Duplicate a challenge card for each student.

GET SET

▶ Arrange the class into nine groups of three or four students.

▶ Ask each group to design a hole using available equipment: cones for obstacles, a carpet for the putting surface, cups for a hole, and so on. The length will be limited by available space.

▶ Students should put their design on paper and share it with the teacher before beginning construction.

GO!

1. Assign each group a starting hole and play a "best ball" format, in which each student hits a shot from the tee.

2. The group determines which shot is best, and they each play a shot from that position.

3. When reaching the putting surface, they determine which ball is in the best position and alternate putts from that position until one is made.

4. The team score is recorded on the scorecard.

Team name: _____

Members: _____, _____, _____, _____

Chip-and-Putt Group Challenge

Hole	Chips	Putts	Total
1			
2			
3			
4			
5			
6			
7			
8			
9			
Total score			

From Jeff Carpenter, 2007, *Physical Education Self-Management for Healthy, Active Lifestyles* (Champaign, IL: Human Kinetics).

Racket Sport Challenges

Pickleball, badminton, and tennis challenge students, but they also can frustrate and discourage them unless they have numerous opportunities to experience small successful steps within the teaching and practice progression. Spending lots of time chasing mis-hit balls is not only frustrating to the teacher but also to students. Presenting a series of activities related to racket sports is one way to challenge and motivate students. As students develop sufficient skills in one activity, they can successfully move to one requiring a higher level of skill. A success-oriented progression begins with pickleball (shorter racket, smaller court, limited ball bounce), followed by badminton (longer, but light, racket; shorter flight on the birdie), and finally ends with tennis (longer, heavier racket; larger court; greater flight or bounce of the ball).

As with the golf activities, before presenting any of the following challenge activities, you must provide appropriate instruction related to grips, swing technique, and body position.

Each of the following challenge activities can be performed with pickleball, badminton, and tennis. As students achieve success with one of the activities—pickleball, badminton, or tennis—demonstrate the differences in technique for another activity. Give them time to practice either individually or in small groups and then move into the challenge activity phase.

GRIP, VOLLEY, AND MOVE CHALLENGE

The Grip, Volley, and Move Challenge provides students the opportunity to practice their skill in a format where group cooperation is essential to success while keeping track of individual progress and setting goals based on personal success.

STANDARDS

▶ Physical Education Standard 1: Demonstrates competency in motor skills and movement patterns needed to perform a variety of physical activities.

▶ Physical Education Standard 2: Demonstrates understanding of movement concepts, principles, strategies, and tactics as they apply to the learning and performance of physical activities.

▶ Physical Education Standard 5: Exhibits responsible personal and social behavior that respects self and others in physical activity settings.

GET READY

▶ Arrange four stations around the facility, as shown in the floor diagram. Provide sufficient space between stations so that students can move back and to the side when necessary without interfering with another student.

▶ Provide enough equipment for each student: a racket and ball or birdie.

▶ At each station provide the required equipment so that students can move from one station to the next without taking the equipment with them. Once students begin to successfully complete the stations with one type of equipment—pickleball, badminton, or tennis—allow them to take the activity-specific equipment with them. Remember, students progress from pickleball to badminton to tennis while the stations remain the same. Everyone should begin with pickleball and progress as far as they can over time.

▶ Prepare a challenge card for each student.

GET SET

Review the forehand and backhand grips and swing patterns with students and allow time to practice without a ball or partner.

◁ GO!

1. Explain the challenge stations and how to record attempts and successes on individual cards.
2. Assign groups of students to each station. On the go signal, students begin their challenge. After 7 to 10 minutes, students rotate stations. Students work in pairs. If enough space or equipment is not available, one group waits while the other practices. Rotate these positions every 3 or 4 minutes.
3. Even if students do not succeed at a station, they still move on. This keeps the frustration and discouragement levels lower. When they return to that station, they use the same piece of equipment—pickleball, badminton, or tennis—that they used the previous time.

◁ STATIONS

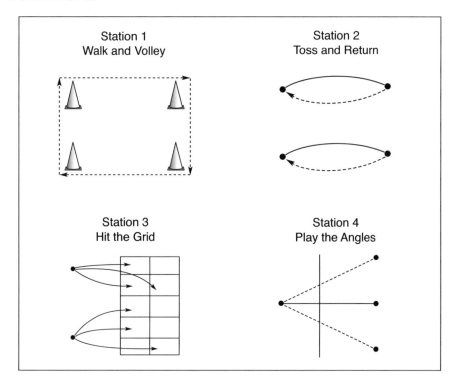

Station 1
Walk and Volley

Station 2
Toss and Return

Station 3
Hit the Grid

Station 4
Play the Angles

▶ Station 1, Walk and Volley—Students slowly walk within a 10 × 10 foot (3 × 3 m) square while maintaining a low and controlled self-volley. Students first use a forehand (underhand) grip 10 times, progress to a backhand (overhand) grip 10 times, then alternating grips for 10 volleys. Students repeat the progression for the duration and record the total number of successful hits.

▶ Station 2, Toss and Return—Two students stand 10 feet (3 m) apart. One student returns an underhand toss directly to his or her partner. For pickleball and tennis, the ball should bounce before the return. After 10 attempts, students reverse roles. Students record the number of hits directly returned to their partner.

▶ Station 3, Hit the Grid—From the hitting zone, students drop the ball (for badminton they toss the birdie in the air) and hit it into one of the grid areas. Their partner catches the ball. Students try to hit a different grid area with each hit. After 10 hits, partners reverse roles. Students record the number of grids successfully hit each time.

▶ Station 4, Play the Angles—From the hitting zone, students drop the tennis ball or pickleball or toss the badminton birdie and hit it to their partner, who is standing 15 feet (4.6 m) away and directly in front of them. The second hit goes to the partner, who is now standing at a 45-degree angle to their left, and the third hit goes to the partner, who is now at a 45-degree angle to their right. Partners reverse roles after 10 hits. Students record the number of hits directly returned to their partner.

Name: _____

Date: _____

Grip, Volley, and Move Challenge

	Attempts	Successes
Walk and Volley		
Toss and Return		
Hit the Grid		
Play the Angles		
Total successes		

From Jeff Carpenter, 2007, *Physical Education Self-Management for Healthy, Active Lifestyles* (Champaign, IL: Human Kinetics).

✁ -

Grip, Volley, and Move Challenge Station 1

Walk and Volley

Complete 10 forehand volleys, 10 backhand volleys, and 10 alternating volleys. Repeat as many times as possible in the time limit.

From Jeff Carpenter, 2007, *Physical Education Self-Management for Healthy, Active Lifestyles* (Champaign, IL: Human Kinetics).

Grip, Volley, and Move Challenge Station 2

Toss and Return

Make 10 attempts to return the ball to your partner, then switch with your partner. Repeat as many times as possible in the time limit.

From Jeff Carpenter, 2007, *Physical Education Self-Management for Healthy, Active Lifestyles* (Champaign, IL: Human Kinetics).

Grip, Volley, and Move Challenge Station 3

Hit the Grid

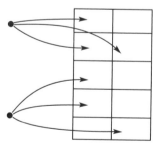

Make 10 attempts to hit the grid, then switch with your partner. Repeat as many times as possible in the time limit.

From Jeff Carpenter, 2007, *Physical Education Self-Management for Healthy, Active Lifestyles* (Champaign, IL: Human Kinetics).

CD-ROM

Grip, Volley, and Move
Challenge Station 4

Play
the Angles

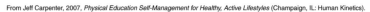

Make 10 attempts to return
the ball to your partner, then
switch with your partner.
Repeat as many times as possible in the time limit.

From Jeff Carpenter, 2007, *Physical Education Self-Management for Healthy, Active Lifestyles* (Champaign, IL: Human Kinetics).

FOUR-SQUARE GROUP RACKET CHALLENGE

This challenge is similar to the playground game of four square and provides a fast-moving activity requiring teamwork, communication, and skill. Rather than attempting to eliminate a person, this activity challenges a group of four to keep the ball in continuous play as long as possible.

Teacher Note

If there are more than four players in a group, one stands behind the server and rotates in after each miss. All players rotate one square to their right, with the player in the square before the server position rotating out.

⌐ STANDARDS

▶ Physical Education Standard 1: Demonstrates competency in motor skills and movement patterns needed to perform a variety of physical activities.

▶ Physical Education Standard 2: Demonstrates understanding of movement concepts, principles, strategies, and tactics as they apply to the learning and performance of physical activities.

▶ Physical Education Standard 5: Exhibits responsible personal and social behavior that respects self and others in physical activity settings.

⌐ GET READY

▶ Set up four-square courts within the facility—one court for every four students. Each court should be a 10 × 10 foot (3 × 3 m) square divided into four equal quadrants.

▶ Place four rackets and one ball or birdie at each location. Set up an equal number of pickleball, tennis, and badminton stations.

▶ Prepare a challenge card for each student.

⌐ GET SET

Arrange students in groups of four and assign each to a playing area. Remind them that to be successful they must keep the ball or birdie in the playing area. The group records the highest number of consecutive hits.

99

◁ GO!

On the go signal, each group begins volleying the ball or birdie. For pickleball and tennis, the ball may bounce only once in each square before it is hit into another square. With badminton, the birdie cannot touch the ground during a volley. After 5 minutes, stop and ask each group for the highest number of consecutive hits they have made. Have them rotate to a different skill court: pickleball to tennis, tennis to badminton, and badminton to pickleball. After groups have rotated through all three skills, ask them which skill they were the most successful with and why.

Team name: _____

Members: _____, _____, _____, _____

Four-Square Group Racket Challenge

Activity	Attempt 1	Attempt 2	Attempt 3	Attempt 4	Best attempt
Pickleball					
Badminton					
Tennis					
Total score (total of all three best attempts)					

From Jeff Carpenter, 2007, *Physical Education Self-Management for Healthy, Active Lifestyles* (Champaign, IL: Human Kinetics).

Bowling Challenges

Bowling is a fun and challenging activity enjoyed by students and adults. In the physical education setting, students can bowl with a commercial indoor bowling set or with liter pop bottles with about 2 inches (5 cm) of sand in the bottom and a small rubber playground ball that can be gripped with one hand. Either way, students learn and have fun while improving eye–hand coordination and learning another lifelong activity.

ALL-STAR BOWLING CHALLENGE

Although bowling does not provide moderate or vigorous levels of physical activity, students do learn to set goals, to challenge themselves, and to receive immediate rewards for their success, which makes it a worthwhile activity. To begin, teach students the three-finger grip, pendulum delivery, and the one-step approach using opposition and provide them practice opportunities. A fun and challenging way to practice these techniques is to divide the class into pairs and position partners 10 feet (3 m) apart. Give a softball or wiffle ball to each student and ask the students to step forward with the foot on the opposite side from the hand holding the ball, bend down, and roll the ball to their partner. Ask students to keep track of how many times out of 10 attempts they successfully roll the ball.

⏄ STANDARDS

▶ Physical Education Standard 1: Demonstrates competency in motor skills and movement patterns needed to perform a variety of physical activities.

▶ Physical Education Standard 2: Demonstrates understanding of movement concepts, principles, strategies, and tactics as they apply to the learning and performance of physical activities.

▶ Physical Education Standard 5: Exhibits responsible personal and social behavior that respects self and others in physical activity settings.

⏄ GET READY

▶ Set up four stations in the facility, each with three bowling lanes. Each lane should have the directed number of pins and one or two balls. Pins should be close to a wall with the start line 20 to 30 feet (6 to 9.2 m) away.

▶ Prepare a challenge card for each student.

⏄ GET SET

Demonstrate each station to the students and remind them of the proper form—some students may use a one-step approach and others may use three or four steps. Regardless of the approach, all students must use good opposition, a pendulum arm movement, and a smooth release. Also remind students that it is not how hard or fast they roll the ball, but the accuracy of the hand direction at release: palm toward the target.

⏄ GO!

Assign students to a station, two students per lane. One partner assumes the bowler position, and the other stands by the pins and is the pinsetter.

As the bowler rolls and knocks down pins, the setter either moves downed pins out of the way or resets the pins and rolls the ball back to the bowler. After the prescribed number of rolls, partners switch positions. Groups spend approximately 5 minutes at each station.

◖ STATIONS

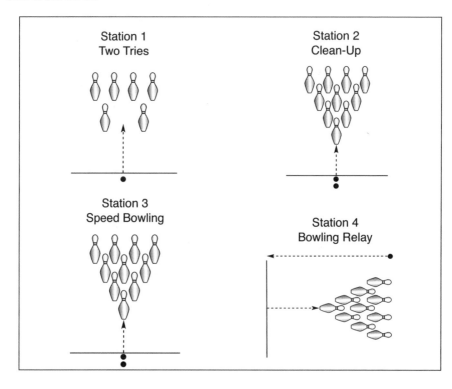

▶ Station 1, Two Tries—Set six pins at the end of each lane. The bowler counts how many pins he or she knocks down after each series of two attempts. Record the total number knocked down while at this station.

▶ Station 2, Clean-Up—Set all 10 pins up at the end of each lane. Both partners stand at the bowling line. The first partner rolls, goes down, and removes downed pins (if all are knocked down, they are all reset). The second partner then rolls the ball and tries to knock down the remaining pins. In succeeding frames, students alternate between the first and second roller. Successes are recorded by the second partner.

▶ Station 3, Speed Bowling—Partners both stand at the bowling line with all 10 pins set at the opposite end. On the go signal, the partners have 5 minutes to see how many pins they can knock down. Each bowler gets two rolls per turn—the other partner runs down, gets the ball, sprints back, and hands the ball to the bowler, who takes his or her second turn. After two turns, students record as successes the total number of pins knocked down. Once the scores are recorded, both partners work together to reset the pins for the next attempt.

▶ Station 4, Bowling Relay—One partner stands at each end of the lane. One pin is set and the bowler attempts to knock down that pin. If successful, the original pin is set back up and another pin is added. Students add pins until there is a miss. At that point, they record the total number of pins knocked down, and partners switch positions. The rotation continues for 5 minutes.

Name: _____ Date: _____

All-Star Bowling Challenge

	Attempts	**Successes**
Two Tries		
Clean-Up		
Speed Bowling		
Bowling Relay		
Total successes		

From Jeff Carpenter, 2007, *Physical Education Self-Management for Healthy, Active Lifestyles* (Champaign, IL: Human Kinetics).

All-Star Bowling Challenge Station 1

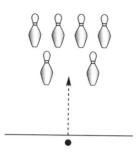

Two Tries

Roll two balls before switching with your partner.

From Jeff Carpenter, 2007, *Physical Education Self-Management for Healthy, Active Lifestyles* (Champaign, IL: Human Kinetics).

All-Star Bowling Challenge Station 2

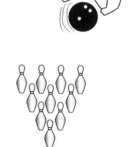

Clean-Up

Alternate rolls with your partner.

From Jeff Carpenter, 2007, *Physical Education Self-Management for Healthy, Active Lifestyles* (Champaign, IL: Human Kinetics).

107

All-Star Bowling Challenge Station 3

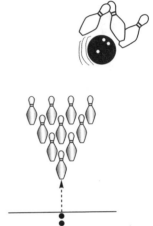

Speed Bowling

Roll two balls before switching tasks with your partner.

From Jeff Carpenter, 2007, *Physical Education Self-Management for Healthy, Active Lifestyles* (Champaign, IL: Human Kinetics).

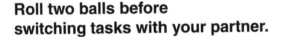

All-Star Bowling Challenge Station 4

Bowling Relay

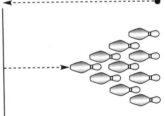

Roll until you miss, then switch tasks with your partner.

From Jeff Carpenter, 2007, *Physical Education Self-Management for Healthy, Active Lifestyles* (Champaign, IL: Human Kinetics).

BOWLING FOR FITNESS CHALLENGE

This activity combines fitness activities and bowling into a fun and challenging format. Be creative with the fitness activities you assign to each frame (see examples) or have groups of students design fitness challenges for each frame.

STANDARDS

▶ Physical Education Standard 1: Demonstrates competency in motor skills and movement patterns needed to perform a variety of physical activities.

▶ Physical Education Standard 2: Demonstrates understanding of movement concepts, principles, strategies, and tactics as they apply to the learning and performance of physical activities.

▶ Physical Education Standard 5: Exhibits responsible personal and social behavior that respects self and others in physical activity settings.

GET READY

▶ Set up enough lanes for four students per lane. Each lane should have 10 pins and one ball. Pins should be close to the wall with the start line 20 to 30 feet (6 to 9 m) away.

▶ Duplicate the Bowling for Fitness Scorecards.

GET SET

Assign students in teams of two to lanes and review the challenge and recording procedures.

GO!

After students have completed 10 frames and all the fitness activities, ask them to design their own fitness activities for each station and play another 10 frames.

Team name: _____

Members: _____, _____

Bowling for Fitness Scorecard

The partners each roll two balls to determine the number of repetitions of each fitness activity they must do. For example, in the first frame, if bowler one knocks down eight pins and bowler two knocks down seven pins, both partners do 15 jumping jacks. Record the number of repetitions in the box below the fitness activity.

Fitness activity	Jumping jacks	Push-ups	Curl-ups	Push-ups	Jump rope	Jumping jacks	Curl-ups	Push-ups	Curl-ups	Jump rope	Total
Repetitions											

From Jeff Carpenter, 2007, *Physical Education Self-Management for Healthy, Active Lifestyles* (Champaign, IL: Human Kinetics).

CHAPTER

4

In-Class
Performance Resources

A day will never be
any more than you make of it.

Decision making, problem solving, and self-direction are essential to the development and implementation of a healthy and active lifestyle. Although students begin their experiences in teacher-directed programs, they soon should begin moving toward a student-directed and self-oriented focus. To make this transition, teachers must give them in-class opportunities and resources to begin the process. The speed of progress depends on each student's readiness to take on these responsibilities.

The activities and resources presented in this chapter provide each student with multiple opportunities to gain new knowledge and learn new skills in addition to monitoring activity and lifestyle patterns. As students complete personal logs, work sheets, projects, and tasks, they must have an opportunity to review and discuss the data with teachers, who will help them make appropriate revisions.

HEALTHY TAG

This activity combines a fast-moving, fun physical activity with learning important information directly related to a healthy lifestyle.

TEACHER HINT

Remind the class that staying in control while moving is the key to safety in any tag game. To add variety, change the locomotor activity: Rather than having students run, instruct them to skip, gallop, or hop. You can also ask students wearing blue to skip, students wearing red to gallop, and students wearing green to run.

STANDARDS

▶ Physical Education Standard 4: Achieves and maintains a health-enhancing level of physical fitness.

▶ Physical Education Standard 5: Exhibits responsible personal and social behavior that respects self and others in physical acitvity settings.

▶ Health Education Standard 1: Students will comprehend concepts related to health promotion and disease prevention to enhance health.

GET READY

▶ Gather three or four foam disks, such as foam Frisbees, or small foam balls.

▶ Duplicate three or four sets of information cards.

GET SET

Have the students find an open space within the boundaries of the basketball court. Designate three or four students to be taggers and four or five students to be rescuers. Give each tagger a foam disk or soft ball. Give each rescuer a set of information cards.

GO!

On the start signal, students begin moving throughout the area. Taggers attempt to tag the other students by touching them with the disk or ball. They cannot throw the object. If tagged, the student stops and begins doing jumping jacks. The rescuers run to the students who have been tagged and ask them a question from an information card. If the student answers correctly, he or she is back in the game. If the student answers incorrectly, the rescuer asks a second question. If the student answers the second question incorrectly, he or she runs to the teacher, asks the teacher the question, gets the correct answer, and returns to the game. After approximately 3 minutes, assign different students to the tagger and rescuer positions.

Teacher Note

Information cards contain a question and an answer related to health and fitness on the same side of the card. Sample questions and answers are provided in this section. These samples can be photocopied and laminated onto index cards.

Aerobic Fitness Information Card

When jogging, walking, swimming, or riding a bike for approximately 20 minutes, what component of physical fitness are you enhancing? (aerobic fitness)

General Knowledge Information Card

Complete this sentence: Physical activity is a good way to improve your _____ and _____. (health and fitness)

Activity Information Card

Give three examples of an active sport and three examples of aerobic activity (active sport—basketball, cross country, tennis; aerobic activity—jogging, swimming, biking)

From Jeff Carpenter, 2007, *Physical Education Self-Management for Healthy, Active Lifestyles* (Champaign, IL: Human Kinetics).

Activity Information Card

Name three sections of the Activity Pyramid. (lifestyle physical activity, aerobic activity, active sports, flexibility, muscular strength and endurance, rest or inactivity)

From Jeff Carpenter, 2007, *Physical Education Self-Management for Healthy, Active Lifestyles* (Champaign, IL: Human Kinetics).

WHAT DO PEOPLE DO?

This is a great activity that combines both knowledge-based and activity lessons that are directly related to developing a personal health and fitness plan. Through this activity, students have an opportunity to survey parents, friends, and neighbors about their activity patterns; analyze the information; discuss conclusions; and gain awareness of various resources and activity patterns.

TEACHER HINT

Remind students to keep accurate records and to stick to the actual questions. Students might ask for or receive additional information from the people they survey, but this information should be written at the bottom of the survey sheet. This information can add a great deal to class discussions about the survey results.

STANDARDS

▶ Health Education Standard 3: Students will demonstrate the ability to access valid information and products and services to enhance health.

▶ Health Education Standard 4: Students will demonstrate the ability to use interpersonal communication skills to enhance health and avoid or reduce health risks.

GET READY

Print copies of the Physical Activity Survey form.

GET SET

Discuss with the class the need to develop individual activity patterns that meet personal needs and goals. Before conducting the survey, students should research and discuss the benefits of physical activity and different ways they are physically active both in and out of school. Discussions should also include their current impressions of what adults and older students within the community may do in order to be physically active.

GO!

Each student should select or be assigned a research partner. Give each student three Physical Activity Survey sheets and ask him or her to survey three different people—family, friends, or neighbors. After the surveys are complete, the partners analyze their data, combine with other groups, and create a community profile. After completing the community profile, the class discusses the findings, draws conclusions, and makes recommendations.

117

Name: _____ Date: _____

Physical Activity Survey

Age: _____   Gender: _____

1. Do you participate in a regular fitness activity program?   ☐ Yes   ☐ No

   If yes, what do you participate in? _____

   _____

   _____

2. Are you physically active but don't participate in a regular fitness activity program?
   ☐ Yes   ☐ No

   If yes, what do you do? _____

   _____

   _____

3. Why is or why isn't physical activity important to you? _____

   _____

   _____

4. Do you participate in physical activity with other people?   ☐ Yes   ☐ No

   If yes, check who they are: ☐ Family   ☐ Friends   ☐ Others

5. Do you believe you are physically fit?   ☐ Yes   ☐ No

6. Additional comments _____

   _____

   _____

   _____

From Jeff Carpenter, 2007, *Physical Education Self-Management for Healthy, Active Lifestyles* (Champaign, IL: Human Kinetics).

LIFESTYLE CHANGES FOR A HEALTHY LIFE

Health and fitness are an important aspect of total wellness. All of us have room to make lifestyle changes that will improve our health and fitness. However, many simple habits that can be modified are often overlooked.

TEACHER HINT

Use this activity before providing opportunities for students to begin tracking their personal health and fitness habits and activities.

STANDARDS

- ▶ Physical Education Standard 5: Exhibits responsible personal and social behavior that respects self and others in physical activity settings.
- ▶ Health Education Standard 6: Students will demonstrate the ability to use goal-setting skills to enhance health.
- ▶ Health Education Standard 7: Students will demonstrate the ability to practice health-enhancing behaviors and avoid or reduce health risks.

GET READY

Review the positive lifestyle activities listed on the sample activity checklist. Adopting these habits can directly affect the development and maintenance of appropriate fitness levels. Add or delete activities from the sample list as appropriate before duplicating one copy for each student.

GET SET

Present the concept of making lifestyle changes, why they are important, the benefits, and so on. Ask the class to suggest changes they can make to positively influence their personal health and fitness. Keep a record of student suggestions and add them to the Health and Fitness Lifestyle Changes Checklist.

GO!

1. Give each student a Health and Fitness Lifestyle Changes Checklist. Ask students to add activities they would like to adopt before filling out the checklist.

2. Write the letters of the alphabet on the board. Divide the class into groups of three or four and assign each group a series of letters (A–G, H–N, and so on). Ask each group to list possible lifestyle changes beginning with each letter in their series. After each group has completed the activity, have members write their changes on the board and discuss the activities and the impact of each on health and fitness.

CD-ROM

Name: _____ Date: _____

Health and Fitness
Lifestyle Changes Checklist

Put an X next to the activities you will consider adopting. If you are not sure, put a question mark in the box and discuss the activity with your teacher, family, and friends.

Lifestyle activities	
Climb stairs instead of using the elevator or escalator.	
When riding in a vehicle with your parents or someone else, ask them to park in the spot that is farthest from your destination and walk to where you are going. You can make this a group activity.	
Do isometric exercises at stoplights or stop signs when riding in a car.	
Walk the dog or a neighbor's dog around the block regularly.	
Ride a bike to school, to the store, or to visit friends.	
Walk or jog to school, to the store, or to visit friends.	
Stretch in bed in the morning and evening while listening to music.	
Wear light wrist or ankle weights while walking, jogging, or doing yard work.	
Other:	
Other:	
Other:	
Other:	

From Jeff Carpenter, 2007, *Physical Education Self-Management for Healthy, Active Lifestyles* (Champaign, IL: Human Kinetics).

120

MAKING HEALTHY DECISIONS

The choices people make each day directly influence their health. People armed with information about how lifestyle affects personal health and wellness can make choices that will reduce their incidence of preventable diseases. During this activity, students should realize that they are making lifestyle decisions and that these choices can be instrumental in developing healthy lifestyle patterns.

⊿ TEACHER HINT

Remind students that they make many decisions each day: what outfit to wear, whom to sit with at lunch, what homework to do first. Each of these decisions is based on information they have received. The key to making responsible decisions is to analyze the choices and choose the option that will result in a positive and healthy outcome.

⊿ STANDARDS

▶ Physical Education Standard 5: Exhibits responsible personal and social behavior that respects self and others in physical activity settings.

▶ Health Education Standard 5: Students will demonstrate the ability to use decision-making skills to enhance health.

⊿ GET READY

Make copies of the Learning to Make Healthy Decisions Handout.

⊿ GET SET

Give one copy of the Learning to Make Healthy Decisions Handout to each student and have the students divide into four groups. This is their first decision.

⊿ GO!

1. Present the Learning to Make Healthy Decisions Handout and discuss it with the class.

2. Ask each student to write down how he or she decided which group to sit with. Ask each group to make a list of the common factors used and then to present the list to the class.

3. Have each group read their list. Write a general list of common factors on the board.

4. Give each group one scenario and tell them to discuss it and decide how best to respond to this problem situation. Each group chooses a recorder and someone to present the group's results to the class.

5. When groups have completed their task, have each group present their situation, the alternatives they considered, how they answered their question, and what decision they recommended.

◁ TEACHER HINT

Everyone is a decision maker. And as people grow older, they make more decisions and more complex decisions. It is important that people make their own decisions based on accurate and current information. Making healthy decisions now will help students avoid unhealthy results later. When presenting each scenario, discuss its relationship to the development, implementation, and maintenance of a healthy lifestyle.

Name: _____ Date: _____

Learning to Make Healthy Decisions

Using the following model as a guide, read through the sample scenario, answer each section, and decide what to do.

Responsible Decision-Making Model

1. Identify the situation.

2. Get the facts—what are the possible alternatives you might consider?

3. Ask questions about possible choices—would the results be any of the following?
   - Healthy
   - Safe
   - Legal
   - Show respect for yourself and others
   - Follow guidelines from parents, guardians, and yourself

4. Make a responsible decision.

5. Develop an action plan.

6. How would you act on your decision?

7. How would you evaluate the results of your decision?

Sample Scenarios

1. You have completed a fitness assessment and found that you are below the healthy zone in aerobic fitness. You want to improve. You would like to join a health club but none of your friends are joining—they jog, ride bicycles, or use the school fitness center after school. What are you going to do?

2. You tend to eat a lot of snack food in the evening when you study. You don't eat much dinner. To maintain a healthy weight and body composition you need to make modifications in your diet. What are you going to do?

3. Friends invite you to a party. At the party some of your friends are drinking beer. A friend keeps asking you if you want to try the beer. At first you say no, but after a while you think to yourself why not? How will you make a healthy and safe decision?

4. Each day after school you usually ride the bus about half a mile (800 m) home, have a snack, and watch TV or play video games. The school has just started an after-school physical activity program that sounds like fun. If you take advantage of this program you know the activity will be healthy—but you will miss your favorite TV show and have to walk the half mile (800 m) home. What process and choices are available to you? What decision will you make?

From Jeff Carpenter, 2007, *Physical Education Self-Management for Healthy, Active Lifestyles* (Champaign, IL: Human Kinetics).

123

STUDY AND ACTIVITY GUIDES

Study and Activity Guides present student-centered tasks that provide an ideal method for helping students connect theory with practical application. Through the use of these guides, students develop approaches to creating personal health, fitness, and activity goals that will lead to a practical lifestyle plan.

Although all students in class will use the same Study and Activity Guides, each student will develop his or her own program to meet personal goals and needs. The use of these Study and Activity Guides involves reading and understanding various questions and writing responses. If students experience difficulty in reading and comprehension, consider using partners or study groups.

TEACHER HINT

Each Study and Activity Guide should be used in conjunction with a related skill and activity-based lesson (e.g., Study and Activity Guide 1 used in conjunction with fitness activities).

STANDARDS

- ► Physical Education Standard 5: Exhibits responsible personal and social behavior that respects self and others in physical activity settings.
- ► Health Education Standard 1: Students will comprehend concepts related to health promotion and disease prevention to enhance health.
- ► Health Education Standard 5: Students will demonstrate the ability to use decision-making skills to enhance health.
- ► Health Education Standard 6: Students will demonstrate the ability to use goal-setting skills to enhance health.

GET READY

Duplicate one Study and Activity Guide for each student. Choose an activity on which to base the class discussions and completion of the Study and Activity Guide.

GET SET

Review the resources that will be available to students and make sure you have arranged time to meet with each student to review and respond to his or her questions.

◀ GO!

After providing a basic overview of the Study and Activity Guide, have students read each section and complete the activities. After students complete the activities, discuss class responses and check for understanding. During the skill and activity portion of the class period, ask students how they were able to use the information they learned from the Study and Activity Guides.

After completing each Study and Activity Guide, let students work with the information for several weeks before they begin keeping track of their lifestyle patterns. This will allow them time to use their new skills and knowledge before moving into the initial application phase.

Teacher Note for Study and Activity Guide 1

Study and Activity Guide 1 provides students a basic understanding of health-related physical fitness. To present this basic information to the class, review each component of health-related fitness—aerobic endurance, flexibility, muscular strength, muscular endurance, and body composition—and provide examples of each. As the students begin to examine their philosophy and activity patterns, provide positive feedback and reassure them that their likes and dislikes regarding specific activities will not affect their ability to reach their goals as long as they are active and they address the components of health-related fitness.

Teacher Note for Study and Activity Guide 2

Begin Study and Activity Guide 2 by defining and discussing lifetime activities. Students generally think only of sports or sport-related activities. In addition to reviewing the data collected on the Physical Activity Survey, presented earlier in this chapter, ask students to speak with family and friends who have graduated from high school about the physical activities they participate in now.

The activity in Study and Activity Guide 2 helps students analyze their habits and current lifestyle. Review Study and Activity Guide 1 and discuss the general concepts for developing a healthy and active lifestyle.

Teacher Note for Study and Activity Guide 3

To be able to develop, implement, and maintain a healthy lifestyle, students need to know what personal health is and how it is important to their personal lives. To make sure all students understand the concepts to be used in this activity, have them brainstorm the basic factors that lead to a healthy lifestyle.

Ask each student to write down what he or she believes the basic factors are. After the students have completed this list, write all the concepts on the board and have students compare and contrast their list to the general list. After this discussion, students are ready to complete their Study and Activity Guide.

Teacher Note for Study and Activity Guide 4

Developing and maintaining a healthy lifestyle includes physical activity and several other positive lifestyle choices. One of these choices is healthy nutritional habits. Although most students have a general awareness of proper nutrition, students need practical experience in making appropriate choices. Before students complete the Study and Activity Guide, review and discuss basic aspects of nutrition and diet.

Healthy eating means taking in the appropriate amount of nutrients each day. The six classes of nutrients are carbohydrate, protein, fat, vitamins, minerals, and water. Give students examples of each and emphasize that the body needs appropriate amounts of each class in order to function in a healthy manner.

Name: _____ Date: _____

Study and Activity Guide 1

Physical Fitness—What Does It Mean?

Your body is like a machine: It requires fuel, cleaning, and maintenance to keep it in top condition and operating properly. Your body's fuel is food. Just like a machine's fuel, your body's fuel must be appropriate and consumed in an amount that keeps the engine running. And like a machine, your body must be maintained. You do this through appropriate and regular exercise and by getting enough rest.

Exercise helps maintain your body by strengthening muscles, burning excess calories, and improving your flexibility. A proper and effective exercise program should become an important part of your regular schedule.

Activity

Describe what exercise means to you. _____

_____

_____

_____

_____

Briefly describe your current level of fitness and physical activity. _____

_____

_____

_____

_____

(continued)

From Jeff Carpenter, 2007, *Physical Education Self-Management for Healthy, Active Lifestyles* (Champaign, IL: Human Kinetics).

CD-ROM

Physical Fitness *(continued)*

When beginning or changing your exercise and activity program, you should do several things.

- Before starting, check with your doctor to find out if you have medical issues that should be considered when planning a new or modified exercise or activity program.
- Make your exercise time fun by working with a friend. Also reward yourself for your accomplishments.
- Choose activities you like. If you don't enjoy the activity, chances are you won't stick with it.

Activity

What is your favorite way to exercise? _____

_____

_____

_____

Why do you like to exercise in this way? _____

_____

_____

_____

Does your way of exercise include the following?

- Frequency: three to five days every week
- Intensity: working at a moderate to high intensity level
- Time: 20 to 30 minutes each time
- Type: an activity that leads to meeting your goals

Is anything missing?

_____

_____

_____

_____

_____

Activity

What would you like to change about your fitness and activity lifestyle?

_____

(continued)

From Jeff Carpenter, 2007, *Physical Education Self-Management for Healthy, Active Lifestyles* (Champaign, IL: Human Kinetics).

Physical Fitness *(continued)*

_____

_____

_____

_____

What would happen if you made this change?

_____

_____

_____

_____

What things, people, or other barriers might get in the way?

_____

_____

_____

_____

What can you do to change these barriers?

_____

_____

_____

_____

Who can help you make these changes?

_____

_____

_____

_____

From Jeff Carpenter, 2007, *Physical Education Self-Management for Healthy, Active Lifestyles* (Champaign, IL: Human Kinetics).

Name: _____ Date: _____

Study and Activity Guide 2

A Lifetime of Fitness and Activity

Participating in regular physical exercise and activities provides many important health benefits. These benefits include the following:

- Physical benefits: the ability to gain, maintain, and improve muscular strength and endurance, flexibility, and aerobic fitness and health

- Social benefits: new friendships, better communication with others, and the ability to feel comfortable in a variety of situations

- Emotional benefits: stress management, increased self-esteem, and increased self-discipline

As people get older they often find it easier to participate in individual rather than group or team activities. The following are reasons for this:

- Work schedules, family responsibilities, and other commitments make group activities difficult to schedule.

- Physical changes, such as decreased flexibility, back stiffness, and decline in agility, make it more difficult to participate in traditional team activities such as football and soccer.

- Individual activities do not require a group in order to achieve success.

- Outside of a school setting, a greater variety of individual activities are available (e.g., swimming, hiking, skiing, tennis, golf).

(continued)

From Jeff Carpenter, 2007, *Physical Education Self-Management for Healthy, Active Lifestyles* (Champaign, IL: Human Kinetics).

Activity 1: Activities for a Lifetime

For each benefit area, complete the sentence and give examples of lifetime activities that a person could participate in.

Physical benefits help people gain, maintain, and improve

_____

_____

_____

_____

_____

Social benefits help people gain, maintain, and improve

_____

_____

_____

_____

_____

Emotional benefits help people gain, maintain, and improve

_____

_____

_____

_____

_____

Other benefits of a lifetime of physical exercise and activity

_____

_____

_____

(continued)

From Jeff Carpenter, 2007, *Physical Education Self-Management for Healthy, Active Lifestyles* (Champaign, IL: Human Kinetics).

_____

_____

Activity 2: Benefits to You

Now that you have thought about various benefits and possible activities, use the following to analyze activities that you like and that you participate in. List three activities and write what you think are the physical, social, and emotional benefits; remember, there can be more than one benefit for each activity.

Activity 1: _____

Physical: _____

Social: _____

Emotional: _____

Activity 2: _____

Physical: _____

Social: _____

Emotional: _____

Activity 3: _____

Physical: _____

Social: _____

Emotional: _____

From Jeff Carpenter, 2007, *Physical Education Self-Management for Healthy, Active Lifestyles* (Champaign, IL: Human Kinetics).

Name: _____ Date: _____

Study and Activity Guide 3

Choices for a Healthy Lifestyle

Making healthy choices and understanding the benefits of each are important in developing a healthy lifestyle. To live a healthy lifestyle you first need to understand what personal wellness is.

Activity 1: Healthy Lifestyles

What do you think a healthy lifestyle is? _____

_____

_____

_____

The following definitions are what others believe personal health and wellness are:

- A healthy lifestyle lets you do what you want and be who you want to be.
- A healthy lifestyle takes in everything you do and gives it meaning.
- A healthy lifestyle takes in everything you are physically, socially, and emotionally.

Think of three different people you know who have developed a healthy lifestyle. What do or did those people do to achieve and maintain a healthy lifestyle?

1. _____

_____

_____

2. _____

_____

_____

3. _____

_____

_____

(continued)

From Jeff Carpenter, 2007, *Physical Education Self-Management for Healthy, Active Lifestyles* (Champaign, IL: Human Kinetics).

CD-ROM

Choices for a Healthy Lifestyle *(continued)*

Activity 2: Reducing the Risks

Factors that lead to the development of a healthy lifestyle include the following:

- Not smoking or using alcohol and other drugs
- Having regular physical checkups
- Acting safely and reducing risk-taking behaviors
- Maintaining appropriate weight and body composition
- Eating a well-balanced diet
- Getting enough rest and sleep each day
- Managing stress and communicating in a clear and positive manner
- Participating in activities that are rewarding

List five things that you believe can help you develop a healthy lifestyle.

1. _____

2. _____

3. _____

4. _____

5. _____

Did you list any of the activities mentioned in the examples? Which ones?

_____

_____

_____

_____

_____

Do you do any of these things now? Which ones?

_____

_____

_____

_____

_____

(continued)

From Jeff Carpenter, 2007, *Physical Education Self-Management for Healthy, Active Lifestyles* (Champaign, IL: Human Kinetics).

Choices for a Healthy Lifestyle *(continued)*

If you are not doing all of them, which ones could you do? _____

_____

_____

_____

_____

Who could help you develop a healthy lifestyle? _____

_____

_____

_____

_____

Activity 3: What Do You Think?

What do you think a healthy lifestyle is? _____

_____

_____

_____

_____

Compare what you now think with what you wrote at the beginning of this Study and Activity Guide. Is anything different? If so, what? _____

_____

_____

_____

_____

How can the information you have learned help you develop, improve, or maintain a healthy lifestyle?

_____

_____

_____

_____

From Jeff Carpenter, 2007, *Physical Education Self-Management for Healthy, Active Lifestyles* (Champaign, IL: Human Kinetics).

Name: _____ Date: _____

Study and Activity Guide 4

Influences on Your Food Choices

In this Study and Activity Guide you will learn about the importance of proper nutrition in leading a healthy life. The first step is to examine the factors that influence your diet and food choices.

Activity 1: Many Influences—Your Choice

Several factors play a role in the food you choose.

- Hunger: Feeling hungry is natural; it is one of the ways your body protects you.

- Culture: Shared customs, traditions, and beliefs influence your choices.

- Family and friends: You choose foods you have grown up with; you eat what your family eats. As you grow older, friends also have a big influence on your habits. For example, when you and your friends go out to eat, you may all order the same pizza with a topping you have never had.

- Emotions: Your feelings can influence your choices, especially food choices. When people are sad or depressed, they may not eat on a regular basis; when they are bored, they tend to eat more.

- Convenience: Busy people may choose foods that are easy to prepare or to get.

- Advertising: Food ads, which seem to be everywhere, influence which foods people buy.

List two examples of how friends influence your food choices.

_____

_____

(continued)

From Jeff Carpenter, 2007, *Physical Education Self-Management for Healthy, Active Lifestyles* (Champaign, IL: Human Kinetics).

Influences on Your Food Choices   *(continued)*

Were these influences positive or negative? Why?

_____

_____

_____

_____

_____

Activity 2: Making a Change

To begin making good choices, you need to learn how to read labels. Check food labels to find out the fat content and the calorie count in a serving. Packaged foods list their weight or volume, the number of calories per serving, the serving size, and the number of calories by grams. The following example shows you how to determine the number of fat calories in a serving of yogurt and what percentage of the serving is made up of fat.

1. Determine the number of calories per gram: 1 gram of carbohydrate = 4 calories; 1 gram of protein = 4 calories; 1 gram of fat = 9 calories.

2. Find the number of calories per serving (on the label).

3. Find the number of grams of fat per serving (on the label).

4. Convert the grams of fat to calories by multiplying the grams by 9 (1 gram of fat = 9 calories).

5. Figure the percentage of fat calories per serving by dividing the number of fat calories by the total number of calories. For example, an 8-ounce container of yogurt contains the following:

   • Total calories: 200

   • Number of servings: 1

   • Number of calories per serving: 200

   • Fat per serving: 4 grams

Do the math: 4 grams × 9 calories per grams = 36 fat calories per serving; 36 fat calories ÷ 200 total calories = 18% fat.

Determine the number of calories and percentage of fat in a serving of regular yogurt and a serving of low-fat yogurt. What is the difference in calories per serving and total percentage of fat?

_____

From Jeff Carpenter, 2007, *Physical Education Self-Management for Healthy, Active Lifestyles* (Champaign, IL: Human Kinetics).

INDIVIDUAL LOGS AND WORK SHEETS: TRACKING YOUR HEALTHY LIFESTYLE

The intermediate grades and middle school are a good time for students to focus on becoming independent and self-directed. This developmental process requires numerous opportunities for students to explore and understand their lifestyle choices, and students in this age group are eager to keep track of their personal habits and patterns.

The role of the teacher is to facilitate student efforts by providing clear explanations, resources, and continual encouragement and support. Because adolescents and preadolescents are self-conscious, it is important that they have an opportunity to meet individually with the teacher to discuss their efforts and to complete a self-analysis of their activities.

◻STANDARDS

▶ Physical Education Standard 6: Values physical activity for health, enjoyment, challenge, self-expression, and/or social interaction.

▶ Health Education Standard 1: Students will comprehend concepts related to health promotion and disease prevention to enhance health.

▶ Health Education Standard 5: Students will demonstrate the ability to use decision-making skills to enhance health.

▶ Health Education Standard 6: Students will demonstrate the ability to use goal-setting skills to enhance health.

◻TEACHER HINT

Before presenting this activity, review the FITT principle.

▶ Frequency: How often you exercise affects the results. Exercise must be done regularly. Most exercise scientists recommend exercising a minimum of three days a week to see improvements.

▶ Intensity: How hard you exercise affects the results. If you can comfortably jog 10 minutes on a flat course, try adding hills or running faster to continue improving.

▶ Time: How long you exercise each time affects the result. Most exercise scientists recommend a minimum of 20 minutes of exercise to yield improvements.

▶ Type: What you do affects the results. Lifting weights benefits muscular strength but not aerobic endurance.

GET READY

Duplicate the appropriate personal logs and work sheets for each student.

GET SET

The role of the teacher is to facilitate, not to direct. The following guidelines provide a proven instructional format.

▶ Provide all students with print and nonprint resources containing appropriate information related to physical activity patterns and healthy lifestyles. In addition, reinforce the importance of physical activity and how maintaining personal logs and journals can be used in the goal-setting process.

▶ Provide clear explanations of how information should be recorded and how you will work with students to analyze data and recommend modifications.

▶ When reviewing student information, provide a variety of positive comments and productive feedback. Have the students analyze physical activity patterns and make modifications that they believe will enhance their efforts.

▶ Ask students to write messages on their logs to remind themselves of things to do, modifications to be made, and personal compliments.

GO!

The saying "Don't put off until tomorrow what you can do today" is a useful thought to keep in mind when developing personal health and fitness plans. As students begin to track their activity patterns, reinforce the need for accuracy and how this information will be used as baseline data in the goal-setting process. Completing logs immediately after the activity not only provides a higher level of accuracy but also provides immediate feedback so that modifications can be made.

Name: _____ Date: _____

Personal Activity Log

Getting the Point

Keep track of your physical activity for four weeks. During that time, set a point goal and try to earn that many points or more. Remember, regular activity is what is important. You cannot make up for a lack of activity during one week with a large amount the next.

In the table that follows is a list of activities you might like to do. Beside each activity is the minimum amount of time you need to spend and the number of points you can earn. To earn the points, you need to be active for the number of minutes listed. If you participate in an activity that is not listed, ask your teacher if it is appropriate and the number of points you might earn.

Activity	Time	Points	Activity	Time	Points
Skiing downhill	20 min	1	Walking slowly	25 min	1
Weight training	30 min	1	Aerobics	20 min	2
Basketball	30 min	2	Cycling	20 min	2
Dancing	30 min	2	In-line skating	20 min	2
Rope skipping	15 min	2	Skating	20 min	2
Skiing cross-country	20 min	2	Swimming laps	20 min	2
Tennis	25 min	2	Volleyball	30 min	2
Walking fast	25 min	2	Jogging	30 min	3

(continued)

From Jeff Carpenter, 2007, *Physical Education Self-Management for Healthy, Active Lifestyles* (Champaign, IL: Human Kinetics).

Getting the Point   *(continued)*

Record your daily and weekly point totals.

Week	Mon	Tues	Wed	Thurs	Fri	Sat	Sun	Total
1								
2								
3								
4								

Personal comments: _____

_____

_____

_____

_____

Teacher comments: _____

_____

_____

_____

_____

From Jeff Carpenter, 2007, *Physical Education Self-Management for Healthy, Active Lifestyles* (Champaign, IL: Human Kinetics).

Name: _____ Date: _____

Tracking Your Day

What Did I Do?

Each day you spend some of your time in physical activity and some of your time being inactive or doing activities that are not truly active. To determine if you are balancing your time appropriately or to find inactive time you could spend being active, record both physical and nonphysical activities and the amount of time you spend in each. Complete one log for each day. On the seventh day, record the information for the day and create a summary for the week in the space provided.

Daily Log

Day of the week:

Time	Activity	Time
6 a.m.–8 a.m.		
8 a.m.–10 a.m.		
10 a.m.–12 p.m.		
12 p.m.–2 p.m.		
2 p.m.–4 p.m.		

(continued)

From Jeff Carpenter, 2007, *Physical Education Self-Management for Healthy, Active Lifestyles* (Champaign, IL: Human Kinetics).

What Did I Do? *(continued)*

4 p.m.–6 p.m.		
6 p.m.–8 p.m.		
8 p.m.–10 p.m.		
10 p.m.–12 a.m.		
12 a.m.–2 a.m.		
2 a.m.–6 a.m.		

Day 7 Summary

Now that you have logged the activities you did and the time spent doing them, determine the intensity using the following examples as a guide.

Inactive	Studying Watching TV Sleeping
Low intensity	Stretching Light weightlifting
Moderate intensity	Walking for 20 minutes Slow jogging for 20 minutes
Vigorous intensity	Step aerobics for 20 minutes Plyometrics

Amount of time spent in vigorous activity _____ and moderate activity _____

Amount of time spent in low-level activity _____ and inactivity _____

Comments: _____

_____

_____

_____

_____

From Jeff Carpenter, 2007, *Physical Education Self-Management for Healthy, Active Lifestyles* (Champaign, IL: Human Kinetics).

Name: _____ Date: _____

Weekly Aerobic Activity Log

To keep FITT, continuous activity counts. Write down your activities, duration, and points. Remember, you must perform some type of activity at least twice in a week to count the points. For example, if you cycle for 30 minutes and jog for 30 minutes, record a total of 5 points.

Points for Tasks

My weekly point goal

Task 5 points each	Time (minimum of 2 times per week)	Task 3 points each	Time (minimum of 2 times per week)
Fast walking	30 min	Slow walking	30 min
Cycling	30 min	Basketball	30 min
Swimming laps	20 min	Tennis	30 min
Skiing cross-country	30 min	Water skiing	20 min
Jogging	30 min	Jogging	20 min
Aerobics class	30 min	Treadmill 4.0 mph	20 min
_____	30 min	_____	20 min
_____	30 min	_____	20 min
_____	30 min	_____	20 min

(continued)

From Jeff Carpenter, 2007, *Physical Education Self-Management for Healthy, Active Lifestyles* (Champaign, IL: Human Kinetics).

CD-ROM

Weekly Aerobic Activity Log   *(continued)*

Keeping Track of My Points

Day	Task	Time	Points	Comment
Mon				
Tues				
Wed				
Thurs				
Fri				
Sat				
Sun				

Total weekly points:_____

Did you meet your weekly point goal? ____ Yes ____ No

If you answered no, what factors kept you from meeting your goal?

_____

_____

Do you need to modify your goals or activities? ____ Yes ____ No

How will you modify your goals or activities?

_____

_____

_____

_____

From Jeff Carpenter, 2007, *Physical Education Self-Management for Healthy, Active Lifestyles* (Champaign, IL: Human Kinetics).

145

Name: _____ Date: _____

Getting Stronger Every Day

The goal for muscular strength and endurance is to have your upper-body, body core, and leg muscles all working together for your health.

Choose your activity and set your goals for week 1.

		Goal		Goal		Goal
Upper body	Push-ups		Pull-ups (choose two grips)		Dips: chair or bench	
Core	Curl-ups		Crunches		Crossover crunches	
Legs	Half squats		Lunges		You choose	

Track your strength workouts and watch yourself get stronger.

Day	Upper-body muscles			Core muscles			Leg muscles		
	Activity	Reps	Sets	Activity	Reps	Sets	Activity	Reps	Sets
Mon									
Tues									
Wed									
Thurs									
Fri									
Sat									
Sun									

Did you meet your goals? _____

What modifications will you make next week? _____

_____

_____

_____

_____

From Jeff Carpenter, 2007, *Physical Education Self-Management for Healthy, Active Lifestyles* (Champaign, IL: Human Kinetics).

146

Name: _____ Date: _____

Exercise Interest Checklist

It is a well-known fact that physical activity provides numerous benefits. However, choosing an activity is not always an easy task. It depends on your fitness level, personal likes and dislikes, what facilities are available to you, and so on. Take an inventory of your current activities and use that information to help you choose future activities.

On your checklist, put an N in the space to the right of activities you do now two or more times each week. Put a P in the box if you are going to continue doing the activity or plan to do it once or twice a week.

Aerobics		Jogging		Swimming	
Basketball		Racquetball		Tennis	
Bowling		Skating		Volleyball	
Cycling		Skiing or snowboarding		Walking	
Dancing		Soccer		Water skiing	
Golf		Softball		Weightlifting	
Hiking		Stretching		Yoga	
_____		_____		_____	
_____		_____		_____	

(continued)

From Jeff Carpenter, 2007, *Physical Education Self-Management for Healthy, Active Lifestyles* (Champaign, IL: Human Kinetics).

CD-ROM

Exercise Interest Checklist *(continued)*

List all of your Ns.   List all of your Ps.

_____   _____

_____   _____

_____   _____

_____   _____

_____   _____

List four activities that you marked with a P that you are not doing now and state how you plan to get started.

1. _____

_____

_____

_____

2. _____

_____

_____

_____

3. _____

_____

_____

_____

4. _____

_____

_____

_____

Name: _____ Date: _____

Lifestyle Changes Checklist

Increasing Awareness and Exploring Options

Nearly everyone has room to make changes in their lifestyle to improve fitness and physical activity levels. Here are some ideas to help you improve your daily routine.

Check those you will consider.

- ☐ Climbing stairs instead of using an elevator
- ☐ When watching TV, exercising during commercials
- ☐ Walking your dog or a neighbor's dog three times a week
- ☐ Riding a bike to school or to visit friends
- ☐ Walking or jogging to the store instead of driving or riding in a car
- ☐ Stretching in bed each morning before you get up and before going to sleep
- ☐ Doing housework or yard work each week
- ☐ Taking part in a recreational sport each week
- ☐ When riding in a car, doing isometric exercises at each red light
- ☐ List another choice: _____
- ☐ List another choice: _____

Write a letter to yourself listing the benefits of each activity you will consider and how it will change and promote your healthy lifestyle. After writing the letter, mail it to yourself and read it to someone when it arrives. Keep track of these activities on your Personal Activity Log. Remember, set reasonable goals and follow the process to evaluate and modify them.

From Jeff Carpenter, 2007, *Physical Education Self-Management for Healthy, Active Lifestyles* (Champaign, IL: Human Kinetics).

149

IMPROVING FLEXIBILITY

Flexibility provides many health benefits. Nearly everything you do from bending to tie your shoe to playing sports requires flexibility. Flexibility is a joint's ability to move through its full range of motion. This range varies from joint to joint.

◁ STANDARDS

▶ Physical Education Standard 4: Achieves and maintains a health-enhancing level of physical fitness.

▶ Health Education Standard 1: Students will comprehend concepts related to health promotion and disease prevention to enhance health.

▶ Health Education Standard 7: Students will demonstrate the ability to practice health-enhancing behaviors and avoid or reduce health risks.

◁ GET READY

▶ Duplicate one work sheet for each student.

▶ Arrange several articles, photos, and illustrations of people participating in various physical activities.

◁ GET SET

▶ Provide each student with a list of physical activities that improve flexibility.

▶ Take a few minutes to discuss each: why and how they benefit flexibility.

▶ Ask students to refer to the articles and visuals when discussing how flexibility is required to perform the activity and how it can be enhanced through the activity.

◁ GO!

Have students complete the activity on the work sheet. (This works well as a homework assignment.) After students have completed the activity, discuss the results of the work sheet. Discussion topics can include common activities; what makes an activity beneficial to flexibility; and which joints, muscles, and connective tissues benefit from a specific activity.

Name: _____ Date: _____

Am I Flexible?

Write a list of the physical activities you now engage in.

1. _____   9. _____
2. _____   10. _____
3. _____   11. _____
4. _____   12. _____
5. _____   13. _____
6. _____   14. _____
7. _____   15. _____
8. _____   16. _____

The following table provides a list of activities that generally improve flexibility. The activities with the most + signs provide the most benefit. Circle the activities found on your list that have more than three + signs. If you have listed activities that do not appear on the following list, discuss their flexibility benefit with your teacher. If you are participating in activities with one or two + signs, are you doing additional flexibility exercises?

(continued)

From Jeff Carpenter, 2007, *Physical Education Self-Management for Healthy, Active Lifestyles* (Champaign, IL: Human Kinetics).

Am I Flexible? *(continued)*

Activity	Flexibility rating	Activity	Flexibility rating
Aerobics	+++	Jogging	+
Archery	+	Martial arts	++++
Backpacking	+++	Racquetball	++
Badminton	++	Rope skipping	++
Baseball	+++	Rowing	++
Basketball	+++	Skating	++
Boating	+	Skiing and snow-boarding	+++
Bowling	++	Soccer	++
Circuit training	+++	Social dance	++
Cycling	++	Softball	++
Dance	++++	Swimming	+++
Football	++	Tennis	++
Golf (walking, swinging)	++++	Walking	+
Gymnastics	++++	Weight training	+++
Handball	+++	Yoga	++++
Hiking	++	Other	

From Jeff Carpenter, 2007, *Physical Education Self-Management for Healthy, Active Lifestyles* (Champaign, IL: Human Kinetics).

BEING MORE FLEXIBLE

To prevent muscles and connective tissue from losing flexibility, people need to stretch regularly and participate in physical activities that improve their flexibility.

STANDARDS

▶ Physical Education Standard 4: Achieves and maintains a health-enhancing level of physical fitness.

▶ Physical Education Standard 5: Exhibits responsible personal and social behavior that respects self and others in physical activity settings.

▶ Health Education Standard 2: Students will analyze the influence of family, peers, culture, media, technology, and other factors on health behaviors.

▶ Health Education Standard 5: Students will demonstrate the ability to use decision-making skills to enhance health.

▶ Health Education Standard 6: Students will demonstrate the ability to use goal-setting skills to enhance health.

▶ Health Education Standard 7: Students will demonstrate the ability to practice health-enhancing behaviors and avoid or reduce health risks.

GET READY

▶ Duplicate one student log per week for each student.
▶ Create a flexibility bulletin board using the results of the Am I Flexible? activity combined with visuals of appropriate and inappropriate stretching exercises.

GET SET

Lead a class discussion reviewing the benefits of flexibility along with concepts focusing on appropriate and inappropriate stretching exercises. Ask students to share flexibility exercises they now do or have seen others do. What parts of the body benefit and what type of physical activities benefit from these exercises?

GO!

Ask students to take their log home, post it in their bedroom, and keep track of their flexibility program by listing the stretching exercises completed in each of the three areas.

153

Name: _____ Date: _____

Favorite Flexibility Exercises

List your three favorite flexibility exercises for the following areas.

Exercises that increase flexibility in your hips, upper leg, and lower leg

1. _____

2. _____

3. _____

Exercises that increase flexibility in your shoulders and arms

1. _____

2. _____

3. _____

Exercises that increase flexibility in your back and core muscle groups

1. _____

2. _____

3. _____

Before beginning any of these exercises, check with your teacher to see if you have chosen exercises that will provide the benefit you want.

Points to Remember

To increase your flexibility you need to participate in activities and exercises that increase your range of motion. Using these logs, keep track of your flexibility activities for four weeks (use a separate log for each week).

- Slow stretching is best and helps prevent injuries. Don't bounce or stretch to the point of pain or discomfort.

- Hold each stretch position for 20 to 30 seconds.

- Breath slowly and deeply. Don't hold your breath.

- Increase the range of motion as you become more flexible over a period of weeks.

Name: _____ Date: _____

I Am Getting Flexible!

Take your log home, post it in your bedroom, and keep track of your flexibility program.

Day	Shoulders and arms	Back and core muscles	Lower body
Mon			
Tues			
Wed			
Thurs			
Fri			

(continued)

From Jeff Carpenter, 2007, *Physical Education Self-Management for Healthy, Active Lifestyles* (Champaign, IL: Human Kinetics). Illustration reprinted, by permission, from NASPE, 2005, *Physical Best activity guide: Middle and high school levels,* 2nd ed. (Champaign, IL: Human Kinetics).

I Am Getting Flexible! *(continued)*

Day	Shoulders and arms	Back and core muscles	Lower body
Sat			
Sun			

What went well?

_____

_____

_____

_____

_____

What did you accomplish?

_____

_____

_____

_____

_____

What will you change for next week?

_____

_____

_____

_____

_____

From Jeff Carpenter, 2007, *Physical Education Self-Management for Healthy, Active Lifestyles* (Champaign, IL: Human Kinetics).

CHAPTER

5

Final Preparations

© Brand X Pictures

The gates of success and personal growth are always open for those who attempt a challenge.

Successful people set goals and develop action plans for accomplishing the necessary tasks. As students begin to develop the self-management skills that will lead toward the development and implementation of a personal health and fitness plan, they must learn the goal-setting process, practice setting goals, and begin to develop strategies for achieving their goals.

Many students don't understand how to set goals. By including several group goal-setting activities and providing clear guidelines and numerous activities for each class, you will allow intermediate grades and middle school level students to learn this important process while having fun and being challenged.

Concepts to Emphasize

- Goals should be specific—Vague or general goals are difficult to accomplish because they provide no clear target.
- Goals should be realistic—Setting goals that are too difficult to achieve leads to failure. Success is important and maintains motivation.
- Goals should be personal—Goals set for reasons other than personal improvement are not usually accomplished. To be successful, students should set goals that are meaningful to them.
- Goals should be assessed and revised—Keeping logs of activities and accomplishments helps students review and determine if they have made appropriate progress. Sometimes a goal is set too high and cannot be accomplished within the specified timeline. If a goal is too difficult to accomplish, the student should modify it.
- Students should participate with a friend—Accomplishing a goal is easier when friends support each other.

One of the first, and sometimes most difficult, steps to developing a healthy and active lifestyle is gaining awareness of the need to make lifestyle changes. The knowledge, skills, and activities presented in previous chapters should help students understand the importance of and need for healthy physical activity. At this point, students should assess their current behaviors and activity levels to determine which areas need the most attention. After this self-assessment, students will begin to develop an action plan that includes realistic goals and schedules. Present the following series of group and individual activities to teach this goal-setting and self-management process.

FITT CHALLENGE

As students begin to plan individual programs, it is important that they understand the FITT principle and how it applies to all activities. The FITT principle states that the frequency, intensity, time, and type of activity a person engages in affects his or her health and fitness level. Depending on the goal, students adjust these components so that the activity can help them reach their goal.

⬜ STANDARDS

▶ Physical Education Standard 4: Achieves and maintains a health-enhancing level of physical fitness.

▶ Health Education Standard 1: Students will comprehend concepts related to health promotion and disease prevention to enhance health.

▶ Health Education Standard 7: Students will demonstrate the ability to practice health-enhancing behaviors and avoid or reduce health risks.

⬜ GET READY

▶ Create a large chart presenting the following definition of the FITT principle and post it on the wall.

▶ Duplicate one FITT Challenge Work Sheet and FITT Challenge Sample Answer Sheet for each group of two students.

⬜ FITT: A Connection for Success

Frequency: how often you engage in the activity

Intensity: how hard you exercise

Time: how long you are active

Type: the type of activity

⬜ GET SET

Review the FITT principle with the students by covering each definition with a sheet of paper and asking students to define each component and give examples. As students correctly define the component, remove the sheets of paper. Ask the class to give examples of how each component applies to their plan.

GO!

Ask students to choose partners and give each pair a FITT Challenge Work Sheet. Instruct each group to discuss and complete the work sheet. Then give each pair the FITT Challenge Sample Answer Sheet and have them compare the activities on it with the activities on their work sheet. Lead a class discussion about the differences in each pair's work sheets and individual programs.

TEACHER HINT

After completing the work sheet assignment, have students try some of the activities they listed. Do they think they could include these activities in their program?

Team name: _____

Members: _____, _____, _____, _____

FITT Challenge Work Sheet

List several types of activities for each health-related fitness component. Then list the recommended frequency, intensity (i.e., light, moderate, vigorous), and time.

Health-related component	Frequency	Intensity	Time	Type (list several)
Aerobic fitness				
Muscular strength				
Muscular endurance				
Flexibility				

FITT Challenge Sample Answer Sheet

Health-related component	Frequency	Intensity	Time	Type
Aerobic fitness	3-7 times per week	Moderate	20-30 min	Walking Jogging Swimming
Muscular strength	3-4 times per week	Moderate to vigorous	30-45 min	Heavy weight-lifting Heavy plyometrics
Muscular endurance	3-7 times per week	Light to moderate	30-60 min	Light weightlifting Resistance-band training
Flexibility	3-7 times per week	Light	20 min	Static stretching

Team name: _____

PREDICT YOUR OUTCOME

The first step in setting a goal is to use accurate information to establish a baseline on which to make decisions. Generally, students perceive their abilities to be greater than they are. Predict Your Outcome is a fun and challenging activity that shows students how to determine a realistic baseline on which they can build achievable goals.

TEACHER HINT

Students tend to predict that they will achieve a much higher level of success than is reasonable. When reviewing the outcome of this activity, emphasize the concept of setting realistic goals based on accurate information. Ask the class what they would predict the outcome of various challenges to be if they were to do this activity another day. How would they determine their predictions?

STANDARDS

▶ Physical Education Standard 1: Demonstrates competency in motor skills and movement patterns needed to perform a variety of physical activities.

▶ Physical Education Standard 2: Demonstrates understanding of movement concepts, principles, strategies, and tactics as they apply to the learning and performance of physical activities.

▶ Health Education Standard 6: Students will demonstrate the ability to use goal-setting skills to enhance health.

GET READY

▶ Set up eight stations around the facility. Stations can correspond to activity and skill development units you are presenting or can consist of unrelated challenges that will enhance skill and fitness levels. Set out enough equipment at each station to allow all students to participate at the same time.

▶ Duplicate one Predict Your Outcome—Goal and Record Sheet for each group.

▶ After explaining the various station tasks, give students approximately 4 minutes to write down what they predict their score at each station will be after 2 minutes of work.

Teacher Note

Because students have not yet attempted or scored these activities, their goals for their first attempt are a true prediction or guess. They don't have an accurate baseline for predicting realistic goals.

163

◁ GET SET

Assign groups of four students to each station. Review how to set realistic group and individual goals. Emphasize that students should continue an activity even if they reach their goal before the allotted time expires. Many students stop when they reach their target. Let them know that exceeding an established goal is desirable and establishes a new baseline to use when setting future goals.

◁ GO!

On the go signal, students begin performing the task at each station. After 2 minutes, give the signal to stop and let students record individual scores. Students will determine team scores after they have completed all stations.

◁ TEACHER HINT

At the conclusion of the activity, ask the class to predict what their scores would be for each activity if they repeat them the next day. Because they now have some idea of their abilities, they have a more accurate baseline on which to develop realistic goals.

◁ SAMPLE STATIONS

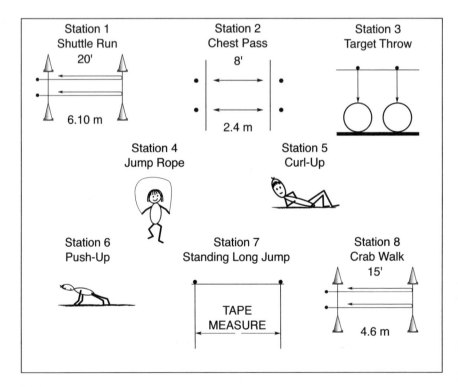

▶ Station 1, Shuttle Run—Set up two parallel lines approximately 20 feet (6 m) apart. Students stand on one line and face the opposite line. On the go signal, students run to the opposite line, touch it with their hand, and immediately return to the other line. Students run back and forth, touching the two lines. The number of lines they touch is their score.

▶ Station 2, Chest Pass—Using a basketball, partners stand approximately 8 feet (2.4 m) apart. On the go signal, they begin passing the ball back and forth using a chest pass. The number of passes made without the ball hitting the ground is the score.

▶ Station 3, Target Throw—Students stand 10 feet (3 m) away from a hula hoop taped to a wall. Students attempt to throw a tennis ball into the target using an overhand throw. The number of throws that hit the target is the score.

▶ Station 4, Jump Rope—Students predict and score the number of times they turn the rope and it passes cleanly under their feet.

▶ Station 5, Curl-Ups—Students predict and score the number of curl-ups they can do with knees bent and hands folded across and against the chest.

▶ Station 6, Push-Ups—From a front support position (with weight supported on the hands and toes), students lower the upper body until the elbows are bent at a 90-degree angle, then they straighten the arms to push back up. Students may perform push-ups from a bent-knee position if appropriate. The number of successful push-ups are scored.

▶ Station 7, Standing Long Jump—Students predict and score the total distance they can jump in 2 minutes. Standing with toes behind a line, students jump forward from both feet as far as possible using a tape measure laid to the edge of the jumping area, measure, and record their distance to the nearest inch, and return to the start line and repeat the movement as many times as they can in 2 minutes. When time is up, they total their distances for a final score.

▶ Station 8, Crab Walk—Set up two parallel lines approximately 15 feet (4.6 m) apart. Students start in a crab-walk position on one line. On the go signal, students begin crab walking toward the opposite line, touch it with their hand, and immediately return to the other line. Students crab walk back and forth, touching each line with their hands before reversing direction. The number of lines they touch is their score.

Members: _____, _____, _____, _____

Predict Your Outcome—
Goal and Record Sheet

Student name	Shuttle Run		Crab Walk		Curl-Ups		Jump Rope	
	Goal	Score	Goal	Score	Goal	Score	Goal	Score
Team total								

Student name	Push-Ups		Chest Pass		Target Throw		Standing Long Jump	
	Goal	Score	Goal	Score	Goal	Score	Goal	Score
Team total								
Team goals and scores (Add individual totals for both rows.)								

From Jeff Carpenter, 2007, *Physical Education Self-Management for Healthy, Active Lifestyles* (Champaign, IL: Human Kinetics). Illustration reprinted, by permission, from NASPE, 2005, *Physical Best activity guide: Middle and high school levels*, 2nd ed. (Champaign, IL: Human Kinetics).

Predict Your Outcome Station 1

Shuttle Run

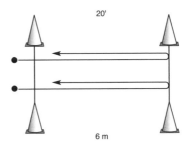

20'

6 m

From Jeff Carpenter, 2007, *Physical Education Self-Management for Healthy, Active Lifestyles* (Champaign, IL: Human Kinetics).

Predict Your Outcome Station 2

Crab Walk

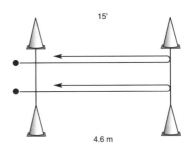

15'

4.6 m

From Jeff Carpenter, 2007, *Physical Education Self-Management for Healthy, Active Lifestyles* (Champaign, IL: Human Kinetics).

CD-ROM

**Predict Your
Outcome
Station 3**

Curl-Ups

✂ -

**Predict Your
Outcome
Station 4**

Jump
Rope

Predict Your Outcome Station 5

Push-Ups

From Jeff Carpenter, 2007, *Physical Education Self-Management for Healthy, Active Lifestyles* (Champaign, IL: Human Kinetics).

Predict Your Outcome Station 6

Chest Pass

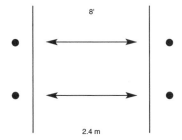

8'

2.4 m

From Jeff Carpenter, 2007, *Physical Education Self-Management for Healthy, Active Lifestyles* (Champaign, IL: Human Kinetics).

Predict Your Outcome Station 7

Target Throw

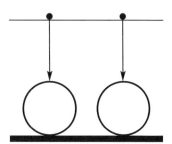

From Jeff Carpenter, 2007, *Physical Education Self-Management for Healthy, Active Lifestyles* (Champaign, IL: Human Kinetics).

Predict Your Outcome Station 8

Standing Long Jump

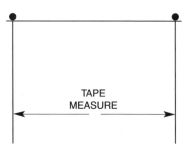

TAPE
MEASURE

From Jeff Carpenter, 2007, *Physical Education Self-Management for Healthy, Active Lifestyles* (Champaign, IL: Human Kinetics).

PREDICT YOUR OUTCOME— THE NEXT STEP

After finishing the initial prediction activity and determining baseline data for each skill, you may want to repeat the activity two more times before moving on to the Next Step. During this activity, students will use their data to set realistic goals. Students should keep their original Predict Your Outcome—Goal and Record Sheet and have it available for the Next Step activity.

⬛ STANDARDS

▶ Physical Education Standard 1: Demonstrates competency in motor skills and movement patterns needed to perform a variety of physical activities.

▶ Physical Education Standard 3: Participates regularly in physical activity.

▶ Health Education Standard 4: Students will demonstrate the ability to use interpersonal communication skills to enhance health and avoid or reduce health risks.

▶ Health Education Standard 6: Students will demonstrate the ability to use goal-setting skills to enhance health.

⬛ GET READY

▶ Set up the facility using the same stations you used in the initial Predict Your Outcome activity.

▶ Duplicate one Predict Your Outcome—The Next Step Goal and Record Sheet for each student.

⬛ GET SET

Review the goal-setting process. Focus on the idea that students should use the baseline information gathered in their previous attempts. Emphasize that by using existing information, they can establish more realistic goals. In setting goals for this activity, students should consider their baseline score and how hard they worked to achieve that score. The question each must ask is, "Did I work as hard as I could to get this score, or can I work a little harder?"

◄ GO!

Using the same groups of four as in the previous activity, assign each group to a station. Give students approximately 4 minutes to determine and write their goals for each station. On the go signal, everyone begins the 2-minute activity.

◄ TEACHER HINT

Repeat this activity regularly. As students become more familiar and successful with the process, change the activities. If you are using this activity as part of a specific unit (e.g., soccer followed by floor hockey then basketball), build two or three fitness activities into each circuit.

CD-ROM

Name: _____ Date: _____

Predict Your Outcome— The Next Step Goal and Record Sheet

List your goal for each activity. After completing an activity, record your score and revise your goal, if necessary. Repeat the activity and record the new goal and explain any differences.

Challenge	1st goal	1st score	New goal	New score	Difference
Shuttle Run					
Crab Walk					
Curl-Ups					
Jump Rope					
Push-Ups					
Chest Pass					
Target Throw					
Standing Long Jump					

Did you meet your new goal? If no, why not? How should your goal be modified next time?

_____

_____

_____

_____

_____

From Jeff Carpenter, 2007, *Physical Education Self-Management for Healthy, Active Lifestyles* (Champaign, IL: Human Kinetics). Illustration reprinted, by permission, from NASPE, 2005, *Physical Best activity guide: Middle and high school levels,* 2nd ed. (Champaign, IL: Human Kinetics).

PYRAMID CHALLENGE

The Pyramid Challenge motivates students to be active every day, both in class and at home. Using this activity before the skill challenges presented in chapters 3 and 5 allows students to begin keeping track of their activity patterns in class before asking them to track activities for an entire day. In addition, it introduces the foundations of a healthy lifestyle reflected in the Activity Pyramid.

STANDARDS

▶ Physical Education Standard 6: Values physical activity for health, enjoyment, challenge, self-expression, and/or social interaction.

▶ Health Education Standard 1: Students will comprehend concepts related to health promotion and disease prevention to enhance health.

▶ Health Education Standard 5: Students will demonstrate the ability to use decision-making skills to enhance health.

▶ Health Education Standard 6: Students will demonstrate the ability to use goal-setting skills to enhance health.

GET READY

▶ Prepare a large chart illustrating the Activity Pyramid (see Pyramid Challenge Activity Pyramid handout) and the basic physical activity guidelines for an active and healthy lifestyle. All students in this age group should be physically active daily as part of general play, games, sports, physical education classes, and recreation.

▶ Duplicate a Pyramid Challenge Activity Pyramid and a Pyramid Challenge Building-Block Pyramid work sheet for each student.

Teacher Note

The Activity Pyramid provided on the handout was developed for teenagers. A poster illustrating an activity pyramid for kids 12 and younger may be purchased at www.HumanKinetics.com.

GET SET

Introduce the concepts and various components of the Activity Pyramid to the class. Focus on the six areas of the pyramid, giving and asking students for examples of activities they engage in that fit in each of the areas. Also introduce how to keep track of their progress toward a goal and record it.

GO!

Give each student a work sheet. The goal is to complete the pyramid within four weeks. For every 20 minutes of activity students complete in a specific area, they place an X in the box. For the first week, keep the work sheets in class. After that, have the students take the sheets home and continue checking off boxes until the sheet is complete. If a student completes the pyramid in less than four weeks, have him or her start a second work sheet.

TEACHER HINT

After the initial four weeks, repeat the activity several times, increasing the time to 30 minutes per activity. Give students an achievement certificate if they complete six blocks per week.

Name: _____ Date: _____

Pyramid Challenge Activity Pyramid

Level 4

Limit Sedentary Living

► Watching TV
► Playing computer games
► Surfing the Internet

Avoid inactive periods of two hours or more during the day (or during waking hours).

Level 3

Flexibility Activities
► Stretching
► Yoga
► Gymnastics

F = 3-7 days/week
I = Moderate stretch
T = 15 to 60 seconds, 1 to 3 sets

Muscle Fitness Activities
► Resistance training
► Calisthenics
► Wall climbing

F = 2-3 days/week
I = Moderate to vigorous resistance
T = 8 to 12 reps, 1 to 3 sets

Level 2

Active Sports and Recreational Activities
► In-line skating ► Canoeing
► Basketball ► Hiking
► Tennis ► Dancing

F = 3-6 days/week
I = Moderate to vigorous (increased heart rate)
T = 20 or more minutes

Active Aerobic Activities
► Biking ► Aerobic dance
► Jogging ► Swimming
► Running ► Treadmill
► Step aerobics ► Stair stepper

F = 3-6 days/week
I = Moderate to vigorous
T = 20 or more minutes

Level 1

Lifestyle Physical Activities
► Walk rather than ride
► Take the stairs
► Do yard work
► Play golf
► Go bowling
► Play active games

F = All or most days of the week
I = Moderate (equal to brisk walking)
T = 30 or more minutes

Accumulate moderate activity from the pyramid on all or most days of the week, and vigorous activity at least three days a week.

Eating well helps you stay active and fit.

From Jeff Carpenter, 2007, *Physical Education Self-Management for Healthy, Active Lifestyles* (Champaign, IL: Human Kinetics). Reprinted, by permission, from C. Corbin and R. Lindsey, 2006, *Fitness for life*, updated 5th ed. (Champaign, IL: Human Kinetics), 64.

Name: _____ Date: _____

Pyramid Challenge
Building-Block Pyramid

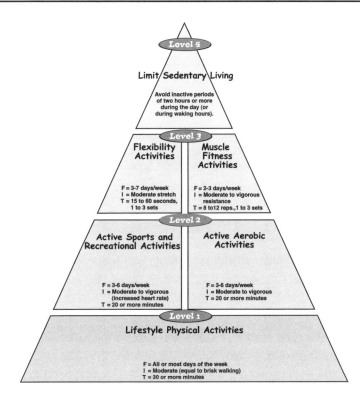

Level 4

Limit Sedentary Living

Avoid inactive periods of two hours or more during the day (or during waking hours).

Level 3

Flexibility Activities

F = 3-7 days/week
I = Moderate stretch
T = 15 to 60 seconds, 1 to 3 sets

Muscle Fitness Activities

F = 2-3 days/week
I = Moderate to vigorous resistance
T = 8 to12 reps.,1 to 3 sets

Level 2

Active Sports and Recreational Activities

F = 3-6 days/week
I = Moderate to vigorous (increased heart rate)
T = 20 or more minutes

Active Aerobic Activities

F = 3-6 days/week
I = Moderate to vigorous
T = 20 or more minutes

Level 1

Lifestyle Physical Activities

F = All or most days of the week
I = Moderate (equal to brisk walking)
T = 30 or more minutes

From Jeff Carpenter, 2007, *Physical Education Self-Management for Healthy, Active Lifestyles* (Champaign, IL: Human Kinetics). Reprinted, by permission, from C. Corbin and R. Lindsey, 2006, *Fitness for life*, updated 5th ed. (Champaign, IL: Human Kinertics), 64.

177

SOFTBALL POINT CHALLENGE

Students are not only motivated to achieve goals they set but also to achieve goals that others set for them. In the following example, a point system is assigned to the activity at each station, and you give students the goal of achieving a total of 1,000 points during the activity. Although the example uses softball skills, you can easily substitute any sport or activity. Remember, create challenging activities to increase a student's motivation while practicing various skills.

⊐ STANDARDS

▶ Physical Education Standard 1: Demonstrates competency in motor skills and movement patterns needed to perform a variety of physical activities.

▶ Physical Education Standard 2: Demonstrates understanding of movement concepts, principles, strategies, and tactics as they apply to the learning and performance of physical activities.

▶ Physical Education Standard 5: Exhibits responsible personal and social behavior that respects self and others in physical activity settings.

⊐ GET READY

▶ Set up eight challenge stations throughout the facility.

▶ Duplicate one Softball Point-Challenge Scorecard for each student.

⊐ GET SET

▶ Review the goal-setting process and explain to students that in some cases, a goal may be set for them by another person.

▶ Separate students into groups of two to four, assign each to a station, and explain each challenge.

⊐ GO!

On the go signal, groups work at their station for 3 to 4 minutes before recording their scores and rotating to the next station.

⊐ SAMPLE STATIONS

▶ Accuracy Throw: Suspend a hula hoop from a basketball rim or from a softball backstop so that it is approximately chest high for students. Standing 20 feet (6 m) away, students throw the ball into the hoop. They can throw underhand or overhand depending on the skill being practiced. (Hint: Put numerous balls in the throwing area.)

▶ Falling Ball: Two partners stand facing each other an arms length from each other. One partner stands on a bench holding a tennis ball or softball. The other partner stands on the ground with hands behind the back. When the student drops the ball, the catcher attempts to catch it. After 10 attempts, the partners switch places. (Hint: Depending on the skill level, two balls may be dropped at one time, and the catcher attempts to catch one in each hand.)

▶ Over the Shoulder: Students stand 3 to 4 feet (1 to 1.2 m) away from a wall, facing it. Students throw a tennis ball at the wall, above head height, immediately turn 180 degrees with their back to the wall, and catch the ball over their shoulder.

▶ Quick Hands: Two students stand 5 feet (1.5 m) away from each other and toss a tennis ball or softball back and forth as quickly as possible.

▶ Ground Ball and Fly Ball: Two students stand 10 feet (3 m) away from each other and throw the ball back and forth. One partner throws fly balls and the other throws grounders. After 10 attempts, they switch roles.

▶ Base Run: Set two bases or cones approximately 30 feet (9 m) apart. Students try to run as quickly as they can between the two bases.

▶ Pepper: Two students stand approximately 6 feet (1.8 m) apart. One partner tosses the ball to the other, who attempts to bunt the ball back. After 10 attempts, partners switch positions.

◁ TEACHER HINT

Have students place their scorecard in a personal health and fitness folder or keep a general file for the cards. After the class has spent some time working to develop these softball skills, repeat this activity. However, before beginning the activity, review how to use previously gathered data and information to set goals. Give the students their completed card, along with a new one, and ask them to write their new goal, based on baseline information, next to the challenge description. After completing the challenge and recording and totaling points, lead a class discussion about positive and negative changes and the possible reasons for the changes and how that data will assist them in setting future goals for this activity.

Name: _____ Date: _____

Softball Point-Challenge Scorecard

Your goal is to earn 1,000 points.

Challenge	Points
Accuracy Throw: 1 point for each successful throw	
Falling Ball: 1 point for each successful catch	
Over the Shoulder: 1 point for each successful catch	
Quick Hands: 1 point for each successful catch	
Ground Ball and Fly Ball: 1 point for each successful catch by both partners	
Base Run: 1 point for each round-trip between bases	
Pepper: 1 point for each successful bunt	

From Jeff Carpenter, 2007, *Physical Education Self-Management for Healthy, Active Lifestyles* (Champaign, IL: Human Kinetics).

GOAL-SETTING PROCESS STUDY AND ACTIVITY GUIDE

The First Step in Your Health and Fitness Plan

After completing several whole-class activities for setting goals, participating in focused activities, reviewing achievement, and modifying goals, it is time for students to start establishing personal health and fitness goals.

STANDARDS

▶ Physical Education Standard 2: Demonstrates understanding of movement concepts, principles, strategies, and tactics as they apply to the learning and performance of physical activities.

▶ Health Education Standard 5: Students will demonstrate the ability to use decision-making skills to enhance health.

▶ Health Education Standard 6: Students will demonstrate the ability to use goal-setting skills to enhance health.

▶ Health Education Standard 7: Students will demonstrate the ability to practice health-enhancing behaviors and avoid or reduce health risks.

GET READY

Duplicate one Student Study and Activity Guide for each student and be prepared to review lessons on the basic goal-setting process.

GET SET

The focus of this Student Study and Activity Guide is to provide students with an understanding of the need to set personal goals and the process involved. At this age, most students have little experience with the goal-setting process and need a lot of assistance when they first begin to develop realistic personal goals. Therefore, before using this guide, you will need to lead the two class discussions outlined in the next section.

GO!

The first discussion relates to the purpose of setting realistic short- and long-term goals and how this process can help individuals and groups achieve a desired outcome. Highlights should include the following:

▶ What a goal is and how it relates to physical activity and health

▶ Definitions and examples of short- and long-term goals

▶ How setting goals can help a person improve

The second class discussion involves the actual goal-setting process. It is during this discussion that details of the process are defined and become clear to the students. The following should be discussed:

▶ Determining a realistic baseline from which to begin

▶ Determining a realistic outcome

▶ Visualizing what it will take to achieve the goal and determining which steps to take.

▶ How to determine if progress has been made

▶ How to determine if the goal has been achieved

After presenting basic information on goal setting and completing the class discussion, give each student a copy of the Student Study and Activity Guide. Have all students read, ask questions about, and discuss the first section.

Name: _____ Date: _____

Student Study and Activity Guide

Setting Goals: Beginning Your Health and Fitness Plan

Activity 1: Let's Get Started

Read the information on goals with a partner and together discuss what you have read. Do either of you have questions? If you do, ask your teacher. Now discuss what you have read with the entire class.

What Are Goals and Why Have Them?

When you are planning for or want something, achieving it can be a goal. It could be passing a test, saving money to buy something, getting in better physical shape, or learning a new activity. Setting a goal is simply defining a specific thing you want, planning a process to achieve it, and doing it. Goals can be personal or for a group. No matter what goal you set, the process used to achieve it will be the same and you will take personal responsibility for making the decisions.

Short- and Long-Term Goals and What Is the Difference?

Short-term goals are set either as part of the process of achieving a long-term goal or actually achieving something in a short period of time. For example, in the process of achieving the long-term goal of getting at least eight hours of sleep each night, you might set the short-term goal of getting to bed at 9:30 tonight.

Long-term goals take more time to achieve and may be achieved by meeting a series of short-term goals. An example of a long-term goal might be to be able to jog 1 mile (1.6 km) without stopping. This long-term goal might be achieved through a series of short-term goals: during the first week walking or jogging a quarter mile (400 m) six out of seven days, during the second week jogging a quarter mile (400 m) three out of seven days and walking two out of seven days, and so on.

(continued)

From Jeff Carpenter, 2007, *Physical Education Self-Management for Healthy, Active Lifestyles* (Champaign, IL: Human Kinetics).

CD-ROM

Setting Goals *(continued)*

To establish meaningful and realistic goals, you need to analyze and clearly understand what you want to accomplish and what you will need to do. The following steps will get you started:

1. The most important step in the process is to begin. If you really want to achieve a goal, you can. If you rely on parents, friends, or a teacher to set a goal or make you do something, most likely you will not accomplish it. You must believe in yourself and your abilities.

2. Knowing your starting point—baseline—is important. If you don't know where you are now, you cannot set a goal to reach someplace different. For example, to set a goal of increasing muscular strength and endurance, you first need to know how strong you are and how much endurance you have now.

3. Set realistic goals. Too often students, and adults, set goals that are not reasonable. If you set a goal that is too difficult, you will most likely fail or give up. The opposite is also true. If you set a goal that is easily accomplished, you will lose interest in the activity. For a goal to be realistic and worthwhile, you must be able to accomplish it through challenging activities.

4. Goals should be specific and measurable. An example of a specific and measurable goal is "To improve my swimming ability so I can swim for 10 minutes without stopping."

5. Write down your goals so you can remember them, visualize them, and refer to them.

6. Make an activity plan for each day. Even if you don't set daily short-term goals, write up a plan for every day.

7. Check your progress regularly to see if you are making progress. If you are not making the progress you want, modify your goal. Remember, the important part of the goal-setting process is to set realistic goals. If you find that a goal is too difficult, make changes but keep the focus on a similar outcome.

Activity 2: Short- or Long-Term

Now that you understand the difference between short- and long-term goals, it's time to set a simple goal. Remember the goals you set in the class fitness and skill activities? Were they short-term or long-term goals?

Set a short-term goal directly related to your personal health and fitness.

_____

_____

_____

_____

_____

Answer the following questions about your goal.

(continued)

From Jeff Carpenter, 2007, *Physical Education Self-Management for Healthy, Active Lifestyles* (Champaign, IL: Human Kinetics).

CD-ROM

Setting Goals *(continued)*

Why is this goal important to you? _____

_____

_____

_____

_____

When do you want to achieve your goal? _____

_____

What are the small steps you will take in achieving your goal?

_____

_____

_____

_____

_____

What will achieving this goal do for you? _____

_____

_____

_____

_____

Activity 3: Success Is Within Your Reach

Now it's time to begin thinking about how you will accomplish your goals. Remember to realistically predict what you will be able to do.

Review the goal you established in activity 2 and answer the following questions.

What will the benefits be of achieving your goal? _____

_____

_____

_____

_____

(continued)

From Jeff Carpenter, 2007, *Physical Education Self-Management for Healthy, Active Lifestyles* (Champaign, IL: Human Kinetics).

CD-ROM

Setting Goals *(continued)*

What is your starting point, or baseline? _____

_____

How will you achieve your goal? _____

_____

_____

_____

_____

What is your timeline? _____

_____

What may keep you from achieving your goal? _____

_____

_____

_____

_____

What will you do when you achieve your goal? _____

_____

_____

_____

_____

_____

Do you need anything else to begin working toward your goal? _____

_____

_____

_____

_____

Have fun and start working to achieve your goal!

From Jeff Carpenter, 2007, *Physical Education Self-Management for Healthy, Active Lifestyles* (Champaign, IL: Human Kinetics).

MY ACTIVITY LOG:
BEGINNING TO KEEP TRACK

One of the first steps to developing self-management and goal-setting skills is to begin keeping track of accomplishments. In this activity, students are given a copy of My Activity Log on which to begin keeping track of their accomplishments. Students can share completed logs with parents and can make them part of student portfolios or notebooks.

STANDARDS

▶ Physical Education Standard 1: Demonstrates competency in motor skills and movement patterns needed to perform a variety of physical activities.

▶ Physical Education Standard 2: Demonstrates understanding of movement concepts, principles, strategies, and tactics as they apply to the learning and performance of physical activities.

▶ Physical Education Standard 3: Participates regularly in physical activity.

▶ Physical Education Standard 4: Achieves and maintains a health-enhancing level of physical fitness.

▶ Physical Education Standard 5: Exhibits responsible personal and social behavior that respects self and others in physical activity settings.

▶ Health Education Standard 6: Students will demonstrate the ability to use goal-setting skills to enhance health.

▶ Health Education Standard 7: Students will demonstrate the ability to practice health-enhancing behaviors and avoid or reduce health risks.

GET READY

▶ Review the various fitness, skill development, and game activities you will present in the next four weeks.

▶ Prepare a copy of My Activity Log for each student based on your plans.

▶ Each week, one day should be left open for an activity of their choice to be done outside of school.

GET SET

To begin, you may list specific activities that can be done on choice days (e.g., walking, jogging, biking, skating, swimming, various sports, yard work).

187

As you progress through the year, add choice days to the week and allow students to add options to the list of activities.

Discuss with students the need to keep track of progress toward a goal. In this activity some of the goals have been set for them, and others have been left for them to set. As students move through the progression toward managing their own lifestyle, they will learn to set goals that reflect their needs.

◁ GO!

During each class period present opportunities for students to complete the task for that day. At the end of the period have students record their information on the log sheet and return it to their portfolio or notebook. If they did not achieve the goal, they should record the number of repetitions or time actually completed and use that as the goal for their next attempt.

Name: _____ Date: _____

My Activity Log

Put an X in the box after you have completed the daily goal. For your choice day, write in the activity you have completed.

Day	Exercise	Completed goal
Week 1 date:_____		
Mon	20 crunches & 10 push-ups	
Tues	Jog 8 min	
Wed	20 crunches & 10 push-ups	
Thurs	Jog 8 min & 10 push-ups	
Fri	Your choice	

Student signature: _____

Week 2 date: _____		
Mon	20 crunches & 10 push-ups	
Tues	Jog 8 min	
Wed	Your choice	

(continued)

From Jeff Carpenter, 2007, *Physical Education Self-Management for Healthy, Active Lifestyles* (Champaign, IL: Human Kinetics).

My Activity Log   *(continued)*

Day	Exercise	Completed goal
Thurs	Play basketball for 20 min	
Fri	Flexibility & 20 crunches	

Student signature: _____

Week 3 date: _____

Mon	25 crunches & 12 push-ups	
Tues	Walk & jog 10 min	
Wed	Play basketball for 20 min	
Thurs	Your choice	
Fri	25 crunches & 12 push-ups	

Student signature: _____

Week 4 date: _____

Mon	Walk & jog 10 min	
Tues	25 crunches & 12 push-ups	
Wed	Your choice	
Thurs	Jog 10 min	
Fri	25 crunches & 12 push-ups	

Student signature: _____

Name: _____ Date: _____

From Jeff Carpenter, 2007, *Physical Education Self-Management for Healthy, Active Lifestyles* (Champaign, IL: Human Kinetics).

SELF-ASSESSMENT: A KEY TO SELF-MANAGEMENT

After setting basic goals, students have gained the knowledge and skill necessary to set personal goals and work toward them. The next step in the progression toward self-management is gaining the ability to realistically assess personal abilities. How students assess their abilities provides insight into how they feel about themselves and how they perceive their abilities. Their beliefs may or may not match their actual knowledge or skill level. However, self-assessment opens an area of discussion critical to developing effective self-management skills.

STANDARDS

- ▶ Physical Education Standard 2: Demonstrates understanding of movement concepts, principles, strategies, and tactics as they apply to the learning and performance of physical activities.
- ▶ Physical Education Standard 5: Exhibits responsible personal and social behavior that respects self and others in physical activity settings.
- ▶ Health Education Standard 6: Students will demonstrate the ability to use goal-setting skills to enhance health.
- ▶ Health Education Standard 7: Students will demonstrate the ability to practice health-enhancing behaviors and avoid or reduce health risks.

GET READY

- ▶ Set up eight stations around the facility using basketball as an example.
- ▶ Prepare a self-assessment scorecard for each student.

GET SET

- ▶ Explain to students that a self-assessment has no right or wrong answers. Instruct them to judge their own abilities and to refrain from comparing their abilities to the abilities of others.
- ▶ Explain each station and answer questions. Most questions will be related to the standard they need to achieve to be successful. At this age, students usually demand a lot of themselves.

191

◀ GO!

1. On the go signal, students begin to perform the activity at each station. After approximately 4 minutes, stop the activity and ask the students to rate themselves.

2. After completing all stations, ask students to analyze their assessment and make changes if necessary.

3. Collect the self-assessment cards and make comments about your assessment of their skills.

4. The next day give back the cards and ask students to compare and contrast their perceptions to yours. Discuss the differences as a group (e.g., How many rated themselves higher than you rated them and how many lower?). Discuss the importance of evaluating one's own knowledge and abilities when planning, managing, and working toward personal goals.

Basketball Self-Assessment Scorecard

Directions

After performing each skill, check the box that tells how you did.

Skill	I can do this really well.	I am pretty good but need more practice.	I need some help and more practice.
Dribbling and switching hands while moving			
Keeping my head up while dribbling			
Passing to my partner with a chest pass			
Passing to my partner with a bounce pass			
Shooting the ball using a one-hand set shot			
Playing defense and staying between my partner and the basket			
Passing to my partner, moving to a different spot, and catching a pass			
Dribbling a figure-8 pattern and changing hands so my body is between the ball and the cone			

With 1 being low and 10 being high, what do you think your overall ability is? Why did you give

(continued)

From Jeff Carpenter, 2007, *Physical Education Self-Management for Healthy, Active Lifestyles* (Champaign, IL: Human Kinetics).

Basketball Self-Assessment Scorecard *(continued)*

yourself this rating?

_____

_____

_____

_____

_____

Teacher comments:

_____

_____

_____

_____

_____

Name: _____ Date: _____

From Jeff Carpenter, 2007, *Physical Education Self-Management for Healthy, Active Lifestyles* (Champaign, IL: Human Kinetics).

CONTRACT GOAL SETTING: INDIVIDUALIZING YOUR PROGRAM

Once students begin to experience success in classroom-based goal-setting activities and achieving personal short-term goals, they should begin expanding their programs to goals that will take longer and will require more effort to achieve. By providing opportunities for students to take responsibility for learning and achieving, you will help them develop a sense of self-management and commitment, which will lead toward development of functional personal health and fitness plans.

STANDARDS

▶ Physical Education Standard 4: Achieves and maintains a health-enhancing level of physical fitness.

▶ Physical Education Standard 5: Exhibits responsible personal and social behavior that respects self and others in physical activity settings.

▶ Health Education Standard 6: Students will demonstrate the ability to use goal-setting skills to enhance health.

GET READY

Before students can set a goal, they must review all of their baseline information and previous goal-setting work: activity patterns, nutritional habits, fitness level, available time, and available facilities and equipment along with personal likes and dislikes. To begin this task, give students a homework assignment of reviewing their previous work to see if patterns exist, if they can think of anything new, or if changes should be made. During this process students may choose new activities or programs to participate in.

GET SET

Prepare an Action Planning Work Sheet and a Student Action Plan for each student.

GO!

Instruct students to complete their Action Planning Work Sheet as a homework assignment. After they have completed it, schedule meetings with each student to discuss his or her plan, goals, and activities. After discussing the plan and asking and answering questions, give the student his or her Student Action Plan. Students will complete the plan as a homework assignment and return it to you for your approval and signature. Once the plan is agreed on, students begin their work. Keep in mind that weekly or twice-weekly checks are necessary to provide continued support and motivation.

CD-ROM

Action Planning Work Sheet

List a personal goal. Then list the ways you will accomplish this goal, what might get in your way, how you will overcome barriers, and who can help you achieve your goal.

State your personal goal.

_____

_____

_____

_____

_____

How will reaching this goal help you?

_____

_____

_____

_____

What will you do to accomplish your goal?

_____

_____

(continued)

From Jeff Carpenter, 2007, *Physical Education Self-Management for Healthy, Active Lifestyles* (Champaign, IL: Human Kinetics).

Action Planning Work Sheet *(continued)*

_____

_____

_____

What could get in your way?

_____

_____

_____

_____

How could you overcome these things?

_____

_____

_____

_____

Which friends and family members will help you?

_____

_____

_____

_____

Name: _____ Date: _____

I will reach my goal by: _____

CD-ROM

Let's Get Started: Student Action Plan

List a specific goal, specific activities you will do to achieve the goal, and how you will measure your progress. Get others who will support you to sign your action plan and commit to helping you.

List your specific goal (remember, your goal must be realistic, achievable, and measurable).

_____

_____

_____

_____

_____

Why is achieving this goal important to you?

_____

_____

_____

_____

List the specific activities you will do (include activities, time, and place).

_____

_____

_____

(continued)

From Jeff Carpenter, 2007, *Physical Education Self-Management for Healthy, Active Lifestyles* (Champaign, IL: Human Kinetics).

Student Action Plan *(continued)*

_____

_____

When and how will you measure your progress (list dates and type of measurement)?

_____

_____

_____

_____

_____

I will support and help you achieve your goal (signed by friends and family members).

_____

_____

_____

_____

Teacher's signature: _____

From Jeff Carpenter, 2007, *Physical Education Self-Management for Healthy, Active Lifestyles* (Champaign, IL: Human Kinetics).

Dress Rehearsal
for a Healthy Lifestyle

*Think big, believe big, act big,
and your results will be big.*

The preadolescent years are a turbulent time. They are also a time when students learn and practice taking more control of their lives. Although parents and teachers continue to make many decisions, it is a time when students begin to understand and take responsibility for lifestyle decisions. As they develop this skill, they continue to need friendly guidance to help refine decisions and enhance knowledge and skills.

Once students have enhanced their knowledge and skills through a program designed to facilitate self-management, it is time to begin developing an initial plan: a personal health and fitness plan. Outlining a step-by-step strategy for achieving preestablished goals is considered a plan. If the plan is based on realistic goals, students will experience success and ensure continued progress toward a healthy and active lifestyle.

However, your job as a teacher does not end when an action plan is written. Use the following guidelines for keeping in touch with students to help them follow through with their plan, make modifications where indicated, and learn new and exciting activities.

- Scheduled follow-up meetings
- Quick informal check-ins (e.g., during passing period or whenever you see a student asking how the aerobic fitness plan is coming and if he or she needs help). Be specific so that students know you are interested in their individual plan.
- Written notes that offer encouragement and information about new resources that become available
- Written notes asking students if they have questions and how they are progressing and requesting a response
- Newsletter articles

Students are interested in the reasons for and the results of regular exercise and good nutritional habits. In helping students to develop a well-designed individual health and fitness plan, provide each student with multiple opportunities to monitor their current activity and nutritional patterns combined with opportunities to enhance their knowledge and skill base related to their personal goals.

Another effective way to continue supporting students, both those previously in your class and those new to it, is to have former students share their plans, successes, and failures. At the beginning of your class, have former students make a presentation and offer their support to the new class. This practice not only helps students but also expands your knowledge by providing information about your program and what modifications you could make to improve your skills and the usefulness of the program.

FINAL ANALYSIS

To begin this activity, review and discuss a variety of the activities and concepts you have presented in the progression. These activities have emphasized the importance of daily physical activity in promoting health and fitness throughout the students' lives. Students must understand the role of physical activity and health in their lifestyle. Students analyze each activity to determine whether they can or cannot use it in their plan.

STANDARDS

▶ Physical Education Standard 5: Exhibits responsible personal and social behavior that respects self and others in physical activity settings.

▶ Physical Education Standard 6: Values physical activity for health, enjoyment, challenge, self-expression, and/or social interaction.

▶ Health Education Standard 1: Students will comprehend concepts related to health promotion and disease prevention to enhance health.

▶ Health Education Standard 5: Students will demonstrate the ability to use decision-making skills to enhance health.

▶ Health Education Standard 6: Students will demonstrate the ability to use goal-setting skills to enhance health.

GET READY

▶ Duplicate a copy of the Study and Activity Guide for a Lifetime of Activity for each student.

▶ Check individual student portfolios when selecting activities that students should review as they develop their plan.

GET SET

Begin this project with a class discussion defining lifetime activities and the benefits gained from participation in them. Generally, students will initially list activities they have participated in during a physical education class or list sport-related activities. Encourage students to think of other types of activities. To help students come up with a more comprehensive list, ask them to research magazines, talk to parents, and so on as part of the study guide activity.

GO!

After the class discussion, students make a list of all the lifetime activities they can think of. Remind students of the definition of lifetime activities and ask leading questions (e.g., "Is playing tackle football a lifetime activity?"). After reviewing the definition and discussing student responses, students begin work on their study and activity guide; this is a great homework assignment.

Give students several days to complete their study and activity guide. Suggest that they speak to their family and friends about the activities they have chosen to see if there are barriers that need to be overcome or lessons to be provided. If there are, how can they overcome the barriers?

CD-ROM

Name: _____ Date: _____

Study and Activity Guide
for a Lifetime of Activity

You're almost there. The following exercises will give you the opportunity to analyze a variety of lifetime activities you might participate in outside of school. When completing these exercises think about the health-related fitness concepts, decision-making skills, and the goal-setting process you have learned.

Activity 1: Activities for a Lifetime

Activities that a person can participate in at almost any age and do not require a team or group of players are considered lifetime activities. Examples include golf, tennis, and swimming. These activities provide physical benefits such as improved aerobic capacity or strength, health benefits such as reduced stress levels, and social benefits such as time with friends or opportunities to meet new friends. Each is important and needs to be considered when making your personal plan.

List two lifetime activities you participate in or would like to participate in.

1. _____

2. _____

(continued)

From Jeff Carpenter, 2007, *Physical Education Self-Management for Healthy, Active Lifestyles* (Champaign, IL: Human Kinetics).

Study & Activity Guide *(continued)*

What are the benefits of these activities?

Physical benefits:

_____
_____
_____
_____
_____

Health benefits:

_____
_____
_____
_____
_____

Social benefits:

_____
_____
_____
_____
_____

What do you need in order to participate in these activities?

_____
_____
_____
_____
_____

(continued)

From Jeff Carpenter, 2007, *Physical Education Self-Management for Healthy, Active Lifestyles* (Champaign, IL: Human Kinetics).

CD-ROM

Study & Activity Guide   *(continued)*

Are there barriers you must overcome?

_____

_____

_____

_____

_____

How will you overcome these barriers?

_____

_____

_____

_____

Will these activities be fun?

_____

_____

_____

_____

Activity 2: Analyze Your Activities

Choose a lifetime activity that you did not list in activity 1 and write down what you believe to be the benefits of participating in this activity. The following is an example using golf:

- Physical benefits—improved flexibility, aerobic fitness, and coordination and balance
- Social benefits—opportunity to play with others, relaxation
- Other health benefits—stress reduction, self-confidence

Activity: _____

(continued)

From Jeff Carpenter, 2007, *Physical Education Self-Management for Healthy, Active Lifestyles* (Champaign, IL: Human Kinetics).

Study & Activity Guide   *(continued)*

Physical benefits:

_____

_____

_____

_____

_____

Social benefits:

_____

_____

_____

_____

_____

Health benefits:

_____

_____

_____

_____

_____

Would you like to learn this activity or participate in it? Why or why not?

_____

_____

_____

_____

_____

Final Projects

The following final projects provide time for students to review what they've learned and then use it creatively in a variety of fun activities. Each project gives students the opportunity to apply the knowledge and skills they have learned throughout the self-management and goal-setting progression.

CREATE A WORKOUT

Creating a personal exercise and activity plan is one of the most important steps a student will take toward maintaining a healthy lifestyle. When developing this plan, students must remember the concepts they have learned: Activities should be fun, available throughout the year, and challenging. They must also require physical activity. Students should also use their knowledge of the FITT principle when designing a meaningful program.

◄ STANDARDS

► Physical Education Standard 1: Demonstrates competency in motor skills and movement patterns needed to perform a variety of physical activities.

► Physical Education Standard 2: Demonstrates understanding of movement concepts, principles, strategies, and tactics as they apply to the learning and performance of physical activities.

► Physical Education Standard 5: Exhibits responsible personal and social behavior that respects self and others in physical activity settings.

► Health Education Standard 2: Students will analyze the influence of family, peers, culture, media, technology, and other factors on health behaviors.

► Health Education Standard 7: Students will demonstrate the ability to practice health-enhancing behaviors and avoid or reduce health risks.

⊔ GET READY

▶ Create a Workout is the first in the series of projects designed specifically to enhance the student's ability to develop functional fitness plans. In this project, write each of the following activities on an index card: step aerobics, fitness stations, sport skill activity, fitness game, dance, and resistance training. Students may also suggest an activity for teacher approval. Include on the card a space for students to list the equipment they will need and diagram the station they will set up.

▶ Give each group one card.

▶ After getting an activity card, the group must plan and present the lesson to the entire class. During the planning process, they will need to consider and plan for equipment, space, arrangement of other students, lesson length, and so on.

⊔ GET SET

Arrange students in groups of four or five, emphasizing that this is a group project and that all members should contribute to the final presentation. Explain that this is a homework assignment, and they will have two days to prepare. Although you will need more than one class period for the presentations, all groups should be ready by the deadline; draw names to determine the order in which groups will present.

⊔ GO!

After distributing the cards to the groups, instruct the students to plan their activity well. They will need to prepare scorecards and set up their station and equipment in advance, every activity needs a slow warm-up and cooldown period, and they must consider the safety of the movement and the activity. All group members must participate in the presentation.

Work with each group to ensure success. At this age, students may forget some of the basics. Check in after the first day to make sure they are working toward a good presentation. Depending on how the groups are working, you might consider extending the due date to allow three or four days of preparation.

Name: _____ Date: _____

Create a Workout

Sample Activities

- Step aerobics
- Fitness stations
- Sport skill activity
- Fitness game
- Dance
- Resistance training
- Other (students choose with teacher approval)

From Jeff Carpenter, 2007, *Physical Education Self-Management for Healthy, Active Lifestyles* (Champaign, IL: Human Kinetics).

Team name: _____ Date: _____

Create a Workout:
Step Aerobics

Create a 10-minute step aerobic activity for the class.

What equipment will you need?

_____

_____

_____

_____

_____

What space will you need?

_____

_____

_____

_____

What will each team member do?

_____

_____

_____

_____

Will you need anything else?

_____

_____

_____

_____

_____

From Jeff Carpenter, 2007, *Physical Education Self-Management for Healthy, Active Lifestyles* (Champaign, IL: Human Kinetics).

Team name: _____ Date: _____

Create a Workout:
Fitness Stations

Create a six-station fitness circuit. Include stations for upper-body, lower-body, and abdominal strength and for aerobic fitness and flexibility. What equipment will you need?

_____

_____

_____

_____

What space will you need?

_____

_____

_____

_____

What will each team member do?

_____

_____

_____

_____

_____

Will you need anything else?

_____

_____

_____

_____

From Jeff Carpenter, 2007, *Physical Education Self-Management for Healthy, Active Lifestyles* (Champaign, IL: Human Kinetics).

214

Team name: _____ Date: _____

Create a Workout: Sport Skill Activity

Create a sport skill station using a leisure activity that the entire class can participate in. Also create an instructional component.

What equipment will you need?

_____

_____

_____

_____

_____

What space will you need?

_____

_____

_____

_____

_____

What will each team member do?

_____

_____

_____

_____

_____

Will you need anything else?

_____

_____

_____

_____

_____

From Jeff Carpenter, 2007, *Physical Education Self-Management for Healthy, Active Lifestyles* (Champaign, IL: Human Kinetics).

Team name: _____ Date: _____

Create a Workout:
Fitness Game

Create a fitness game using either aerobic fitness or muscular endurance as your theme. Remember to develop a game that everyone in the class will be able to participate in.

What equipment will you need?

_____

_____

_____

_____

What space will you need?

_____

_____

_____

_____

What will each team member do?

_____

_____

_____

_____

Will you need anything else?

_____

_____

_____

_____

From Jeff Carpenter, 2007, *Physical Education Self-Management for Healthy, Active Lifestyles* (Champaign, IL: Human Kinetics).

Team name: _____ Date: _____

Create a Workout: Dance

Create a dance activity for the entire class to participate in. This activity can relate to aerobic fitness, but it must also present specific rhythmic patterns.

What equipment will you need?

_____

_____

_____

_____

_____

What space will you need?

_____

_____

_____

_____

_____

What will each team member do?

_____

_____

_____

_____

_____

Will you need anything else?

_____

_____

_____

_____

_____

From Jeff Carpenter, 2007, *Physical Education Self-Management for Healthy, Active Lifestyles* (Champaign, IL: Human Kinetics).

CD-ROM

Team name: _____ Date: _____

Create a Workout: Resistance Training

Create a resistance training activity for the class using resistance bands, weights, or partner resistance activities.

What equipment will you need?

_____

_____

_____

_____

What space will you need?

_____

_____

_____

_____

What will each team member do?

_____

_____

_____

_____

_____

Will you need anything else?

_____

_____

_____

_____

From Jeff Carpenter, 2007, *Physical Education Self-Management for Healthy, Active Lifestyles* (Champaign, IL: Human Kinetics).

Team name: _____   Date: _____

Create a Workout: Other Activity

Create a fitness game or skill-development activity for the class. You may choose the specific focus, but remember that everyone in the class must be able to participate in it.

What is the activity's focus?

_____

_____

_____

_____

_____

What equipment will you need?

_____

_____

_____

_____

_____

(continued)

Create a Workout   *(continued)*

What space will you need?

_____

_____

_____

_____

_____

What will each team member do?

_____

_____

_____

_____

_____

Will you need anything else?

_____

_____

_____

_____

_____

From Jeff Carpenter, 2007, *Physical Education Self-Management for Healthy, Active Lifestyles* (Champaign, IL: Human Kinetics).

CAN I HELP?

Support and help while working toward a goal or accomplishing a task are helpful and often provides the feedback necessary for someone to achieve a goal. People can give either direct or indirect support. Direct support occurs when people work together during an activity to reach the same goal. A person can provide indirect support by giving feedback, positive or negative, and encouragement to help someone focus and move toward his or her goal. Most often teachers and coaches provide indirect support through feedback, instruction, and encouragement. Peers and family members often provide direct support by buying equipment, providing transportation, paying fees, and so on. The following activity provides students the opportunity to support a friend trying to achieve a goal.

STANDARDS

▶ Physical Education Standard 5: Exhibits responsible personal and social behavior that respects self and others in physical activity settings.

▶ Physical Education Standard 6: Values physical activity for health, enjoyment, challenge, self-expression, and/or social interaction.

▶ Health Education Standard 4: Students will demonstrate the ability to use interpersonal communication skills to enhance health and avoid or reduce health risks.

▶ Health Education Standard 8: Students will demonstrate the ability to advocate for personal, family, and community health.

GET READY

Duplicate one Can I Help?: Helping a Friend Achieve His Goal work sheet for each student. As part of the class discussion, provide examples of how students can be supported, such as direct and indirect examples of how people can help others achieve goals.

GET SET

Discuss with the class that to successfully accomplish a goal, people need the support of a friend or family member who can help them stay on track and focused on their goal. In this activity, students will try to help a friend meet his or her goal. Also, review the FITT principle and its important role in meeting fitness goals.

Spread this activity over two or three days. During the first class period, spend approximately 10 minutes reviewing the FITT principle and the importance of a support network in meeting goals. During the second period, pass out the work sheets, read the scenario about a friend named Jon who wants help creating an exercise action plan, and discuss the different issues he faces. After the discussion, assign the remainder of the work sheet (developing Jon's action plan) as homework.

◻ TEACHER HINT

Although you could grade this activity, I suggest using it only to check for understanding of the FITT principle and elements of the planning process. If a student does not demonstrate an appropriate level of understanding, give a review assignment. Refer to activities in previous chapters related to the FITT principle, goal setting, decision making, and program planning.

◻ GO!

Each day after the class discussions about the work sheet, instruct students to take it home and begin building Jon's plan. After the first day, ask students how they are doing and if they have questions. Before the students turn in the work sheets, ask them to check their action plans using the following information about the FITT principle and an action plan.

FITT Principle Review and Application

Each FITT component is listed and accurately described:

▶ Frequency refers to how often an activity is done; most exercise physiologists recommend three to seven days per week.

▶ Intensity refers to…and so on

A description of how each FITT component is applied is provided:

▶ Frequency. In a beneficial activity program, healthy activities are done on a regular basis.

▶ Intensity. In a logical and healthy progression, a person gains benefits as he or she works harder.

Jon's Action Plan

Jon's action plan addresses two components of health and fitness: aerobic fitness and nutrition and body composition. When developing his activity plan, his current condition and nutritional habits should be considered as well as his goal: participating in a hike with his family in three months.

▶ Two activities for aerobic fitness are listed. Using Jon's present physical condition, the appropriate level of activity is used for each concept.

▶ Two activities for nutrition and body composition are listed. Based on Jon's current nutrition habits, the action plan should address a reduction in specific areas, such as drinking pop, eating ice cream before bed, and eating french fries. Although the FITT components do not directly apply to nutritional habits, they should still be addressed. In the second activity, a link to exercise should be made.

Team name: _____ Date: _____

Can I Help?: Helping a Friend Achieve His Goal

Scenario

Because of your knowledge and skill, Jon, a good friend, has asked you to help him design a plan to help him achieve a specific fitness goal. Jon has made a commitment to himself and his family to increase his aerobic capacity so he can hike 10 miles around Lake Summit, which has some hilly areas, with them during a planned outing in three months.

Jon is a little overweight and rides his bike slowly around the neighborhood on weekends. In his physical education classes, he rarely jogs or engages in activities at a moderate level. He drinks about three cans of pop each day, loves french fries and potato chips, and eats a large dish of ice cream every night before bed. Can you help Jon?

The first thing Jon has asked for help with is the FITT principle. He remembers hearing something about it in his physical education class but can't remember much about it. Since you will be hiking and Jon's aerobic fitness is low, you suggest activities to improve this area.

Component of the FITT principle	Description
Frequency	
Intensity	
Time	
Type	

(continued)

From Jeff Carpenter, 2007, *Physical Education Self-Management for Healthy, Active Lifestyles* (Champaign, IL: Human Kinetics).

Can I Help? *(continued)*

Now that you have reviewed the components of the FITT principle with Jon, he wants to know how they can help him reach his goal and improve his health and fitness levels.

Component of the FITT principle	How can it help? (Use general ideas to explain the concept to Jon.)
Frequency	
Intensity	
Time	
Type	

Jon now has a better understanding of the FITT principle. Help him create an action plan that is realistic, achievable, and measurable. Remember, two areas need attention: aerobic fitness and nutrition and body composition.

On the following chart, list two aerobic fitness activities. Fill in the other FITT principle components to create an action plan. Remember to consider Jon's baseline information and that you do not need to use all components of the FITT principle in each activity.

Jon's Aerobic Fitness Action Plan

Activity 1

Frequency: _____

Intensity: _____

Time: _____

Type: _____

(continued)

From Jeff Carpenter, 2007, *Physical Education Self-Management for Healthy, Active Lifestyles* (Champaign, IL: Human Kinetics).

Can I Help? *(continued)*

Activity 2

Frequency: _____

Intensity: _____

Time: _____

Type: _____

Jon's Nutrition and Body Composition Action Plan

Activity 1

Frequency: _____

Intensity: _____

Time: _____

Type: _____

Activity 2

Frequency: _____

Intensity: _____

Time: _____

Type: _____

From Jeff Carpenter, 2007, *Physical Education Self-Management for Healthy, Active Lifestyles* (Champaign, IL: Human Kinetics).

MAKING THE MOST OF MY COMMUNITY

Once students leave school, they must rely on community resources if they want to continue participating in various activities. Generally, their knowledge and experience with these resources are limited. They may not know about available facilities and programs, their cost, and their restrictions. This activity helps students discover resources that will meet their individual needs.

STANDARDS

▶ Physical Education Standard 5: Exhibits responsible personal and social behavior that respects self and others in physical activity settings.

▶ Health Education Standard 3: Students will demonstrate the ability to access valid information and products and services to enhance health.

▶ Health Education Standard 6: Students will demonstrate the ability to use goal-setting skills to enhance health.

GET READY

▶ Duplicate an activity work sheet for each student and a list of various community resources available to students.

▶ Post a list of the health and fitness professionals in your community you have discovered during previous lessons, including people who have come into the school or have indicated that they would be willing to help students. After seeing the student list, you might want to contact people on that list to let them know that students might contact them and to offer your assistance to their program.

GET SET

Review previous activities using community resources, especially those that apply to resources available in your community for this age group (e.g., bowling alleys, golf courses, ski areas, tennis courts, jogging trails). Emphasize the fact that in order to implement an ongoing health and fitness plan, students cannot rely solely on school-based resources because these usually are not available during vacations or after students graduate.

Spread this activity over several days. During the first session, spend approximately 10 minutes reviewing the importance of awareness and use of community resources. During this session ask students if they have or are currently using community resources. Create a revised list of resources including those not previously listed but used by students. Copy enough lists for each student and hand them out during the next session. During the second session, hand out the work sheets, answer questions, and tell students that they have three days to complete this homework assignment. Remember to check their progress daily and ask if they have questions or have learned anything new about their community.

GO!

After the second class discussion, students begin completing the work sheet as homework. On the due date, collect all work sheets and, as students discuss and share what they have discovered, make a class chart listing the various resources students plan to use or would like to use, for what purpose, and who will use them. Encourage students with similar goals or students using the same resource to pair up for support, cooperation, and fun.

Name: _____ Date: _____

Using My Resources

Think of two healthy-lifestyle goals, one directly related to fitness and the other related to a lifetime activity. Analyze your goals, what you will have to do to accomplish them, what facilities and equipment are necessary, and how you will use community resources to accomplish your goals.

What are your goals?

1. _____

2. _____

What will you do to accomplish these goals?

Goal 1:

_____

_____

_____

_____

_____

_____

(continued)

From Jeff Carpenter, 2007, *Physical Education Self-Management for Healthy, Active Lifestyles* (Champaign, IL: Human Kinetics).

CD-ROM

Using My Resources *(continued)*

Goal 2:

_____

_____

_____

_____

_____

_____

What resources do you need to meet your goal?

Goal 1:

_____

_____

_____

_____

_____

Use the following table to help you decide which community resource you will use to reach goal 1. List resources that could help you meet your goal and answer the questions in each column.

Possible resource	Cost	Equipment needed	Transportation (how to get there)	Instruction and supervision	Age appropriate
Example: Sun City Golf Course	Daily fee: $25 Lessons: $20 each	Clubs; I have some	My sister will take me. She works nearby.	Golf professional	Yes; other kids my age go there.

(continued)

From Jeff Carpenter, 2007, *Physical Education Self-Management for Healthy, Active Lifestyles* (Champaign, IL: Human Kinetics).

Using My Resources   *(continued)*

What resources do you need to meet your goal?

Goal 2:

_____

_____

_____

_____

_____

_____

Use the following table to help you decide which community resource you will use to reach goal 2. List resources that could help you meet your goal and answer the questions in each column.

Possible resource	Cost	Equipment needed	Transporta- tion (how to get there)	Instruction and supervision	Age appropriate
Example: Sun City Golf Course	Daily fee: $25 Lessons: $20 each	Clubs; I have some	My sister will take me. She works nearby.	Golf profes- sional	Yes; other kids my age go there.

Before going on, review your research to see if you have found barriers that cannot be resolved: too expensive, not appropriate for your age group, and so on. If you find barriers, is there an alternative, do you need to do more research, or does your goal need modification? Draw your own grid and repeat this activity as many times as necessary until you find a good resource or ways to eliminate the barriers.

Now that you have found community resource options, it is time to make a plan. The following infor- mation outlines your plan for each goal.

(continued)

From Jeff Carpenter, 2007, *Physical Education Self-Management for Healthy, Active Lifestyles* (Champaign, IL: Human Kinetics).

Community Resources You Will Use—Goal 1

What community resource will you use? _____

How many days or hours will you use this resource? _____

How will you get there? _____

If you must pay a fee, how will you get the money?_____

Who is the adult who will supervise your activity?_____

Are there other considerations? _____

Community Resources You Will Use—Goal 2

What community resource will you use? _____

How many days or hours will you use this resource? _____

How will you get there? _____

If you must pay a fee, how will you get the money?_____

Who is the adult who will supervise your activity?_____

Are there other considerations? _____

Now that you have completed your research and decided which resources will help you meet your goals, it is time to take action. During the next few class periods, your class will discuss what everyone plans to do. If you find a classmate using the same resources, work with him or her. Remember, having another person working with and supporting you helps you achieve your goal.

From Jeff Carpenter, 2007, *Physical Education Self-Management for Healthy, Active Lifestyles* (Champaign, IL: Human Kinetics).

LET'S MAKE A PLAN: IT'S YOUR LIFE SO MAKE THE MOST OF IT

In the preceding lessons, students have learned many skills they can use to develop a personal health and fitness plan. It's now time for them to use this information as they go through the steps of developing their action plan. If their plan is set up properly, they will experience success quickly and ensure progress toward their goals. When working with students in the intermediate grades or in middle school, it is important to remind them that the plan they are about to develop is the first step in a long-term process. As they grow, their interests, abilities, and opportunities will change, which will require changes in their plan. However, their ability to use the knowledge and skills they have just learned will allow them to continue on a path of success and health.

As a teacher, it is your job to lend continual support as your students work toward achieving an active and healthy lifestyle. Although your support is important as students begin their journey, it is also required throughout the process. Your support and assistance will go a long way toward keeping them on track and determined to take control of their lifestyle.

◁ STANDARDS

▶ Physical Education Standard 6: Values physical activity for health, enjoyment, challenge, self-expression, and/or social interaction.

▶ Health Education Standard 5: Students will demonstrate the ability to use decision-making skills to enhance health.

▶ Health Education Standard 6: Students will demonstrate the ability to use goal-setting skills to enhance health.

▶ Health Education Standard 7: Students will demonstrate the ability to practice health-enhancing behaviors and avoid or reduce health risks.

◁ GET READY

Discuss the guidelines for developing a personal health and fitness plan: Determine a baseline for health-related fitness, activity patterns, and nutrition habits; set realistic, achievable, and measurable goals; select enjoyable physical activities to participate in; and determine who can help and support the plan and activities. At this point, it is important to reinforce the concept that personal health and fitness are personal matters. Students should not compare themselves to anyone else when working toward self-improvement. You should also point out that one of the biggest contributors to success is attitude. Students with a good attitude try to remain focused and on track and don't let others influence them in a negative way. A positive attitude makes a tremendous difference in all areas of life. As Thomas Jefferson said, "Nothing can stop people with the right mental attitude from achieving their goals."

GET SET

Duplicate one copy each of the Fitness Planning Work Sheet and My Personal Health and Fitness Plan for each student.

GO!

After reviewing the concepts of baseline data and the FITT components along with the components of health-related fitness, give the students their planning sheets. Allow two or three days to complete this phase of the process. When plans are completed, individually review them, make comments and suggestions, and move to the next phase, My Personal Health and Fitness Plan.

Name: _____   Date: _____

Fitness Planning
Work Sheet

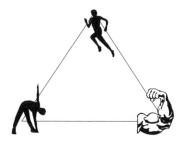

Your physical education class is about to end and you want to continue your efforts to stay active, enhance your fitness level, and get ready to play on a school team next fall. You have actively taken part in a physical education class and have learned how to develop a plan. You have already made plans to hike, swim, and play on a team this summer, but you want to work on your physical fitness.

Your plan will focus on three of the components of health-related fitness: aerobic fitness, muscular strength and endurance, and flexibility. For each of these components you need to develop a plan.

1. To begin, review your previous fitness scores for each component—your baseline information.

2. Next, determine whether you are above, below, or within the *FITNESSGRAM* healthy zone for each component.

3. Finally, determine whether your goal should focus on maintenance or improvement in each component.

(continued)

From Jeff Carpenter, 2007, *Physical Education Self-Management for Healthy, Active Lifestyles* (Champaign, IL: Human Kinetics).

CD-ROM

My Current Health-Related Fitness

Health-related fitness component	Baseline— current level	Within, above, or below the healthy zone	Improvement or maintenance needed
Example: aerobic fitness	PACER test score: 31 (13-year-old girl)	Within	Improvement
Aerobic fitness			
Muscular strength & endurance			
Flexibility			

Now that you have determined your health-related fitness baseline, it's time to create an action plan specifically designed to meet your goals. Using the FITT principle, list how you will maintain or improve your fitness to reach your goal in each component area using activities you have chosen.

Aerobic Fitness Goal

	Goal	Activity
Frequency		
Intensity		
Time		
Type		

Muscular Strength and Endurance Goal

	Goal	Activity
Frequency		
Intensity		
Time		
Type		

(continued)

Fitness Planning Work Sheet   *(continued)*

Flexibility Goal

	Goal	Activity
Frequency		
Intensity		
Time		
Type		

Now that you have completed a plan, review it. Have you accurately determined a baseline of fitness in each component area, accurately selected a goal based on this baseline, and listed activities that you can realistically do? Are your goals measurable? If your answer to any of these questions is no, revise your plan before beginning.

Remember, when implementing your plan, periodically check your progress to determine if you are succeeding. Record the data and make changes in your plan if you need to. Also, just before school begins next fall, do a final check to see if you reached your goals.

When will you begin work on your action plan? _____

Who helped and supported you? _____

When did you complete your plan? _____

Were you successful? _____ Yes _____ No

Explain why or why not.

_____

_____

_____

_____

_____

From Jeff Carpenter, 2007, *Physical Education Self-Management for Healthy, Active Lifestyles* (Champaign, IL: Human Kinetics).

DEVELOPING YOUR PERSONAL HEALTH AND FITNESS PLAN

Now is the time for students to use the knowledge and skills gained through their previous experiences. This is their culminating project.

STANDARDS

▶ Physical Education Standard 2: Demonstrates understanding of movement concepts, principles, strategies, and tactics as they apply to the learning and performance of physical activities.

▶ Physical Education Standard 4: Achieves and maintains a health-enhancing level of physical fitness.

▶ Physical Education Standard 5: Exhibits responsible personal and social behavior that respects self and others in physical activity settings.

▶ Physical Education Standard 6: Values physical activity for health, enjoyment, challenge, self-expression, and/or social interaction.

▶ Health Education Standard 2: Students will analyze the influence of family, peers, culture, media, technology, and other factors on health behaviors.

▶ Health Education Standard 3: Students will demonstrate the ability to access valid information and products and services to enhance health.

▶ Health Education Standard 5: Students will demonstrate the ability to use decision-making skills to enhance health.

▶ Health Education Standard 6: Students will demonstrate the ability to use goal-setting skills to enhance health.

▶ Health Education Standard 7: Students will demonstrate the ability to practice health-enhancing behaviors and avoid or reduce health risks.

GET READY

Throughout this progression, you have encouraged students to develop and maintain an active lifestyle. You have presented a range of physical activities, sports, and exercise routines. You have carefully planned each of these activities to help students develop an initial health and fitness plan.

To begin the final lesson in this progression, provide each student with all work sheets, logs, journals, fitness data, and other recorded information they have collected. Give each student several copies of the planning sheet. (It is a good idea to keep these records in a folder for each student so you can give them back to the student during this lesson).

237

GET SET

Remind students that exercising and leisure-time activities do not have to be work. They should be enjoyable and effective ways to stay physically active throughout their life. Whether they enjoy swimming, biking, golf, jogging, dance, or other activities, any of these are great ways to stay active and fit.

GO!

After reviewing the process for developing a plan and allowing time for students to review their personal information, give them copies of the activity 1 work sheet—Fitness Planning Work Sheet.

Hand out copies of My Personal Health and Fitness Plan. Review the Activity Pyramid, giving examples in each component area. Give students an opportunity to discuss various activities, community resources, and realistic activities. After completing the reviews and discussions, instruct students to begin working on their plan as homework.

After two or three days, students bring to class a draft of their plan. Review the sheets with students individually, checking for realistic goals and activities. While you are reviewing sheets with individual students, the other students can be working on lead-up games or skill activities. Provide feedback to help the students develop a final plan. You can repeat this step several times before students develop their final plan.

When students have finalized their plan, review it with them. During this review, provide encouragement and support their efforts. Remember, this is their plan.

TEACHER HINT

To prepare for this final step in the progression, it is helpful to contact parents, other teachers, and administrators. Each is an important part of the student support network. If other teachers and administrators ask students how they are doing and show an interest in their plan, it has a tremendous impact on a student's motivation. Parents and other family members are especially important because they, most likely, will help with the implementation of the plan by providing transportation and supervision.

Your professional and personal commitment to health and physical activity helps you motivate students to achieve patterns that will lead to a healthy lifestyle. More important, you want students to develop a positive attitude that values health, fitness, and physical activity and allows them to set positive goals and manage their actions as they try to achieve those goals. You can do this by demonstrating motivational skills, a positive attitude, and a genuine appreciation for the individual student.

Name: _____   Date: _____

My Personal Health and Fitness Plan

Using the Activity Pyramid along with all of your baseline information as a guide, you are now ready to develop your own personal health and fitness plan. This plan will be your starting point for building a healthy and active lifestyle.

From Jeff Carpenter, 2007, *Physical Education Self-Management for Healthy, Active Lifestyles* (Champaign, IL: Human Kinetics).

Name: _____ Date: _____

Activity Pyramid

Level 4

Limit Sedentary Living

▶ Watching TV
▶ Playing computer games
▶ Surfing the Internet

Avoid inactive periods of two hours or more during the day (or during waking hours).

Level 3

Flexibility Activities

▶ Stretching
▶ Yoga
▶ Gymnastics

F = 3-7 days/week
I = Moderate stretch
T = 15 to 60 seconds, 1 to 3 sets

Muscle Fitness Activities

▶ Resistance training
▶ Calisthenics
▶ Wall climbing

F = 2-3 days/week
I = Moderate to vigorous resistance
T = 8 to 12 reps, 1 to 3 sets

Level 2

Active Sports and Recreational Activities

▶ In-line skating ▶ Canoeing
▶ Basketball ▶ Hiking
▶ Tennis ▶ Dancing

F = 3-6 days/week
I = Moderate to vigorous (increased heart rate)
T = 20 or more minutes

Active Aerobic Activities

▶ Biking ▶ Aerobic dance
▶ Jogging ▶ Swimming
▶ Running ▶ Treadmill
▶ Step aerobics ▶ Stair stepper

F = 3-6 days/week
I = Moderate to vigorous
T = 20 or more minutes

Level 1

Lifestyle Physical Activities

▶ Walk rather than ride
▶ Take the stairs
▶ Do yard work
▶ Play golf
▶ Go bowling
▶ Play active games

F = All or most days of the week
I = Moderate (equal to brisk walking)
T = 30 or more minutes

Accumulate moderate activity from the pyramid on all or most days of the week, and vigorous activity at least three days a week.

Eating well helps you stay active and fit.

From Jeff Carpenter, 2007, *Physical Education Self-Management for Healthy, Active Lifestyles* (Champaign, IL: Human Kinetics). Reprinted, by permission, from C. Corbin and R. Lindsey, 2006, *Fitness for life,* updated 5th ed. (Champaign, IL: Human Kinetics), 64.

CD-ROM

Name: _____   Date: _____

My Baseline Information

Health-Related Fitness Monitoring

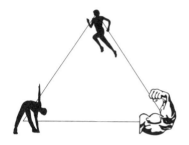

		Date: _____ Ht: _____ Wt: _____	Date: _____ Ht: _____ Wt: _____	Date: _____ Ht: _____ Wt: _____
PACER	Laps			
	FITNESSGRAM healthy fitness zone			
Push-ups	Score			
	FITNESSGRAM healthy fitness zone			
Curl-Ups	Score			
	FITNESSGRAM healthy fitness zone			

(continued)

From Jeff Carpenter, 2007, *Physical Education Self-Management for Healthy, Active Lifestyles* (Champaign, IL: Human Kinetics).

241

Fitness Monitoring *(continued)*

		Date: _____ Ht: _____ Wt: _____	Date: _____ Ht: _____ Wt: _____	Date: _____ Ht: _____ Wt: _____
Sit and reach	Right leg			
	Left leg			
	FITNESSGRAM healthy fitness zone right leg			
	FITNESSGRAM healthy fitness zone left leg			
Trunk lift	Score			
	FITNESSGRAM healthy fitness zone			
Alternative assessment (list here)	Score			
	FITNESSGRAM healthy fitness zone			
Alternative assessment (list here)	Score			
	FITNESSGRAM healthy fitness zone			

Are you in the healthy fitness zone for each of the assessments? _____ Yes _____ No

Note: Alternative assessments could include a mile run (1.6 km) for aerobic fitness, pull-ups for muscular strength, or any other standard fitness assessment. Keep this information to use in monitoring your plan.

From Jeff Carpenter, 2007, *Physical Education Self-Management for Healthy, Active Lifestyles* (Champaign, IL: Human Kinetics).

Name: _____

Date: _____

My Goals

Use the Activity Pyramid to set goals in each area.

What are your overall health and fitness goals?

_____
_____
_____
_____
_____

Date accomplished: _____

What lifestyle activities will you do?

_____
_____
_____
_____

What active sports will you do?

_____
_____
_____
_____

What planned exercise will you do?

_____
_____

(continued)

From Jeff Carpenter, 2007, *Physical Education Self-Management for Healthy, Active Lifestyles* (Champaign, IL: Human Kinetics).

My Goals   *(continued)*

_____

_____

How will you use nutrition and diet to achieve your goal?

_____

_____

_____

_____

How will you reduce risk-taking behaviors?

_____

_____

_____

_____

How will rest and inactivity become part of your plan?

_____

_____

_____

_____

Comments:

_____

_____

_____

_____

From Jeff Carpenter, 2007, *Physical Education Self-Management for Healthy, Active Lifestyles* (Champaign, IL: Human Kinetics).

Name: _____ Date: _____

My Measured Goals

Remember to measure your progress based on your baseline information, your goals, and your action plan.

How did you measure each of your overall health and fitness goals?

_____

_____

_____

_____

_____

How did you measure your lifestyle activity?

_____

_____

_____

_____

How did you measure your participation in active sports?

_____

_____

(continued)

From Jeff Carpenter, 2007, *Physical Education Self-Management for Healthy, Active Lifestyles* (Champaign, IL: Human Kinetics).

My Measured Goals   *(continued)*

_____

_____

_____

How did you measure your planned exercise goal?

_____

_____

_____

_____

How did you measure the effect of nutrition and diet on achieving your goal?

_____

_____

_____

_____

How did you measure the effects of risk reduction?

_____

_____

_____

_____

How did you measure the effects of rest and inactivity?

_____

_____

_____

_____

(continued)

From Jeff Carpenter, 2007, *Physical Education Self-Management for Healthy, Active Lifestyles* (Champaign, IL: Human Kinetics).

My Measured Goals   *(continued)*

Comments:

_____

_____

_____

_____

_____

How Did You Do?

Did you achieve all of your goals?

If yes, which ones?

_____

_____

_____

_____

If no, which ones?

_____

_____

_____

_____

_____

What was difficult about the goals you did not achieve?

_____

_____

_____

_____

_____

(continued)

From Jeff Carpenter, 2007, *Physical Education Self-Management for Healthy, Active Lifestyles* (Champaign, IL: Human Kinetics).

My Measured Goals   *(continued)*

What can you do to achieve your goals, or how can they be modified?

_____

_____

_____

_____

_____

At this point, you have completed the progress and have begun to implement your personal health and fitness plan. As you move toward continuing a healthy and active lifestyle, remember what you have learned about setting goals, including the components of the FITT principle, measuring your progress, and giving yourself rewards for all your accomplishments and continued effort. Keep up the good work!

From Jeff Carpenter, 2007, *Physical Education Self-Management for Healthy, Active Lifestyles* (Champaign, IL: Human Kinetics).

About the Author

Jeff Carpenter, MS, is supervisor of health, fitness, and athletic programs at Olympia School District in Olympia, Washington. In 34 years as a physical educator he has taught at all grade levels—elementary through university. He has authored four other books and numerous professional articles and presented more than 25 sessions at national AAHPERD conferences.

Carpenter has been a consultant to more than 20 school districts throughout the country on physical education curriculum and program development, implementation, and assessment. He helped develop Physical Best and Fitnessgram curricular programs. Carpenter is an instructor for both Physical Best and Fitness for Life and has served as chair for Physical Best and as president of the Washington Alliance for HPERD.

Carpenter has received numerous awards, including Administrator of the Year for Physical Education in 2002 from AAHPERD/NASPE and an Honor Fellow Award from AAHPERD. He also received a President's Honor Award in 1997. In his leisure time, he enjoys golfing, skiing, and sailing.

How to Use the CD-ROM

System Requirements

You can use this CD-ROM on either a Windows®-based PC or a Macintosh computer.

Windows

- IBM PC compatible with Pentium® processor
- Windows® 98/NT 4.0/2000/ME/XP
- Adobe Reader® 8.0
- Microsoft® PowerPoint® Viewer 97 (included)
- 4x CD-ROM drive

Macintosh

- Power Mac® recommended
- System 9.x or higher
- Adobe Reader® 8.0
- Microsoft® PowerPoint® Viewer OS9 or OS10 (included)
- 4x CD-ROM drive

User Instructions

Windows

1. Insert the Physical Education Self-Management for Healthy, Active Lifestyles CD-ROM. (Note: The CD-ROM must be present in the drive at all times.)
2. Select the "My Computer" icon from the desktop.
3. Select the CD-ROM drive.
4. Open the "start.pdf" file.

Macintosh

1. Insert the Physical Education Self-Management for Healthy, Active Lifestyles CD-ROM. (Note: The CD-ROM must be present in the drive at all times.)
2. Double-click the CD icon located on the desktop.
3. Open the "Start.pdf" file.

For customer support, contact Technical Support:

Phone: 217-351-5076 Monday through Friday (excluding holidays) between 7:00 a.m. and 7:00 p.m. (CST).

Fax: 217-351-2674

E-mail: support@hkusa.com